Sex, Drugs, Rock and Roach
Cedric's Story

Michael Flynn

Sad and Happy Days

COOL DAY BOOKS

This book is a work of fiction. Any resemblance to persons living or deceased, is accidental.

Published by Cool Day Books, London
CoolDayBooks@outlook.com
2015

©2015 Cool Day Books

All rights reserved.

ISBN 978-0-9933050-0-9

Printed and distributed by CreateSpace

1

The first erotic pleasures that I remember, were innocent things. I remember as a small child of four or five years old, discovering delightful tingly feelings in my willy when lying face down in bed one morning with the sun streaming through the window. I'll call it my 'willy' because that's what us kids called them in those days. My Mum and Dad somehow managed to refer to it without calling it anything at all! Unsurprisingly then, I quickly sensed that it was something very private that dwelt in a frisson too delicate to withstand the comparative vulgarity of being referred to directly. It was OK to be dried by my parents at bath time. At that age I felt I belonged to them more than to myself. But by inference, they impressed upon me that my willy was my own business, and maybe the doctor's if anything went wrong with it. Beyond that, my parents dealt with it with impeccable modesty, in the same way that poohs and farts were somehow acknowledged and ignored at the same time. Only a real stinker might depart from this norm, usually provoking a merry amalgam of protests and guffaws. It was all very safe and secure, and I look back on it with great fondness.

On another occasion, I dreamt that a woman who lived across the back yard from our house, was sat in a wash basin, her breasts naked and exposed, and each of her nipples protruding from its circular brown surround. Having been breastfed, I suppose my infant mind must have constructed this image from the memory of my mother's breasts, and from my actual acquaintance with the woman across the yard. It was a very strong dream, and a major discovery of sexual desire. I am making a deliberate distinction here, between erotic pleasure and sexual desire, for here the connection of genital pleasure with the image of a naked woman, made an indelible mark on my mind. Once, my friend Brendan and I licked each other's tongues to see what it felt like. It felt nice, very intimate and sensual, what I'm sure Freud would have identified as erotic, but it didn't feel sexual, unlike the dream I have recounted to you, which made me feel I wanted to burst out of my willy for that woman, and was the beginning of what I recognise as my present sexuality.

I grew up around stockinged legs. My Mum, like most women at that time, wore skirts or dresses and nylons. I wasn't very old when I began getting erections at the sight of her putting on her stockings – seven or eight maybe – and I wasn't much older when I began to feel revolted by her effect on me. The fashions of the time favoured skirt lengths just on the knee, and my Mum's skirt, she being rather plump, used to ride up revealingly. I felt disgusted and pleased at the same time by her indiscretion, and suffered greatly from it. I'm quite sure there was nothing malicious in it, except perhaps a selfish single-mindedness in her wish to be attractive. Mainly, I think, she was just naïve to the point of stupidity, or intentional yet unconscious ignorance, and simply had no appreciation of the possibility of there existing in her sphere of experience, either incestuousness or sexual desire in young boys. Eventually, when I was around eleven, my father, who was more canny in this respect, cautioned her saying, "These lads are growing up you know!" She shrugged it off, thinking his reprimand ridiculous. But he had seen the way my brother and I looked at her, and knew better. It was a relief to know that he'd noticed, but it didn't come soon enough to prevent a deep ambivalence towards my mother developing. I hated her for making me feel pleasures and desires that skewed with her being my mother, things that could only be felt by making them impersonal, so that one might desire a glimpse of thigh, while ignoring who it belonged to. To make matters worse, she was getting fat, and I couldn't cope with the mixture of sexual excitement and repulsion that I felt for her.

There were experiences with girls too. I used to play doctors and nurses with my friend Angela. She'd take down her knickers and let me examine her with my toy stethoscope. There was no penetration. Such a thought would never have occurred to me at that age. She just let me see and touch, so I did, and thought it was very interesting how different girls were to boys. I felt as much fascination as pleasure as I recall, and was drawn to the mystique of femininity – I was going to say, "Like a moth to a lamp", but that's far too frenetic. Rather, it was a slow, deeply focused absorption, like the inexorable unfolding of a dream one becomes immersed in. Of course the sensuality that I brought to these experiences was a constant in my life, whether it was the smell and glint of the beads of tar that seeped up out of the road surface on a sweltering hot summer's day, or the pungent stink of dog muck smeared on a sandal in a park shrubbery during exuberant carefree play.

At the age of eight, I fell helplessly in love with the sister of my best friend. To me she was angelic, and I longed for her with all my heart and all my mind. It's funny how as a young child you are able to immerse yourself in all your experiences, and yet let go of them just as easily. That's how it had been with all of the sexual and erotic encounters I had had up until then. And so I never thought about my new sweetheart's private parts. I just loved her face and her voice and her girlish figure. All I wanted was to be with her, and feel the sweet thrill of her presence. One darkening evening we hid in the bushes in an unbuilt plot, and kissed each other on the cheek. I have never since known a more passionate moment. Every night I cherished the thought of her before going to sleep, and very often I couldn't sleep for want of her.

There was a time when Eros came upon us quite unexpectedly. We boys and girls on the street had formed our own little gang, and made small blue membership cards for all the members. One evening, some impish mind hit upon the grand idea of the boys and girls taking it in turn to show themselves to each other. My beloved was one of the girls. Down in a friend's cellar, where her parents had let her make a den, we boys stood in a row and took out our willies while the girls watched. Mine was so stiff I could hardly get it out, and the other boys were quite surprised to see it like that. I just thought that was what mine was like, and I suppose they came to the same conclusion too, for they soon shrugged and took it as 'one of those things', the way kids would, even if they came upon a Martian walking down the street. Anyway, then it was the girls turn. But June, my heart's desire – my heart is singing as I think of this even now, fifty years later – would only show herself to *me*. We went into a corner and she took down her knickers. I dutifully and reverently bent down to look, but couldn't see much in the cellar's gloom. I thanked her appreciatively anyway, and made a date to see her in the park the following Saturday. I retain a vision of us in my mind, playing enthusiastically around a tarpaulin near the swings, me showing off and full of myself, she shouting, "I want my Cedric!" But when Saturday came, my Mum announced that we were going to town to buy some shoes. I begged and pleaded with her not to go, but she was deaf to all my protests and put her foot down. I didn't feel able to tell her why I felt as I did as I sensed the impending disaster. I didn't see June on the street that evening or the next day. At school on Monday I tried to catch her attention, but it was obvious that the spell had been broken. She ignored me, and the following Saturday went off with another boy to the afternoon matinee at the local cinema. But I was loyal and true, and forlornly held her in my heart for two more aching years.

Once in those sad and happy days, one of my friends found a discarded magazine that had been stuffed into the middle of a bush in some waste ground. It was full of black and white photos of women in various states of undress. Their breasts were naturally large and heavy, and they kept their high heels and stockings on. It was very exciting to see. I'm not sure what happened to the magazine after that. It was 'finders keepers' and I wasn't the finder. But I began to notice the men's magazines in the paper-shop my brother and I called into on the way to the swimming baths on Saturday afternoons. We'd go in to buy sweets and bacon-flavoured crisps, but now that I knew what was in those magazines their allure was irresistible, and I'd pick one off the shelf hoping no one would notice, and leaf through it. We wouldn't look for long for fear of receiving an embarrassing telling off by the sales girl, but ah, what sights we beheld!

I began to notice sex in more and more places. My Dad was a keen photographer, semi-professional. Apart from his own personal interests, he charged a small fee to photograph weddings, and was very good at it. His hobby meant we often went into photographic shops. One day while I was marvelling at the 'X-ray' shoe sizing machine, I noticed a revolving rack in the corner loaded with packs of cine-film. Each thin white cardboard carton had a black silhouette on it of a glamorous scantily clad woman. I could hardly take my eyes off it and always tried, 'accidentally on purpose', to meander towards it, but my Dad was always there, and I could never get a good look. And while I think of it, I note how primed I was by then – I was ten or eleven – to want to get a good look. I think now that there was no wrong in having felt such a strong interest in such provocative sexuality. It's quite obvious to me now that I had an intensely sexual and erotic nature from a very early age. Even just peripherally, children are deeply and passionately interested in everything that grown-ups do. They play all the time at being adults in various situations. Sex and war are matters of life and death, so it isn't surprising that children have such a proper and irrepressible interest in both of these. But in my case I think sexual desire awoke early in my life, and that I would have been happier and healthier in my attitudes towards sex, if there had not been as many things around me to continually provoke my interest. Those things led me to grow in a certain direction, which I think it would have been better not to have grown in. True, there were other factors too, but this one was the central and most direct cause of the gradual malformation of my soul that no one either noticed or apparently considered a serious possibility. This seems strange on reflection, as that was the time of the 'Moors Murders' when the drawn and sulky faces of Ian Brady and Myra Hindley stared out from all the newspapers. They looked like children caught red-handed being cruel to an animal, except their victims were children. Their terrifying dead-pan eyes were all the evidence needed of a subterranean world of private interests and desires, that shouldn't see the light of day, and which for us came on top of a series of stories of too imaginable cruelty: a gang of boys, who'd strung up a rabbit by the hind legs above a camp fire and burnt it alive; an old man, who'd chopped a dog up and cooked it in his oven – which was tantamount to cannibalism to us children who knew dogs as pets, each with its own personality. Some years later, I was reminded once again of that same impenetrable opacity of obsessive cruelty, when I found a dog lying by the roadside with dull yellow flames engulfing its prostrate body.

We lived only a few miles from where the Moors Murders were committed, and on learning of them, our parents became prickly with apprehension, warning us of dark and unspeakable dangers lurking beyond the boundaries of sensible obedience and good behaviour. They never knew how near to becoming a reality their fears had already come. One day in a park at the edge of our town, which sat in a valley with a wood on one side and was bordered along the top by a disused railway track, there was a fête with a colourful military display. While our mums were milling around chatting, and four of us boys were off playing, we were approached by an older rather odd looking young man. He had one of those faces that looks a bit deranged, maybe showing signs of brain damage. He very skilfully lured us into the wood and up onto the railway track. Two of my younger friends became sensitive to the danger we were in, and ran off. My remaining friend and I, thought our friends were being silly, and carried on towards a viaduct where the track spanned an intersecting valley. Something happened then, I can't quite remember what. Did he dare us to climb onto the parapet? It may have been that. It's vague now. But whatever it was, it led to him telling us we could run away, which we did, but as we scrambled down the embankment he began to throw large stones at us. I don't know whether he intended to miss or not, but he missed anyway. And we escaped, thinking surprisingly little of it. We didn't even tell our parents what had happened. Yet when I think of it now, and I realise how close pure malice came to us that day, my blood runs cold. I'm sure I speak for my old childhood friends now, when I say that the circumstances of Jamie Bulger's murder, held no surprises for us. Evil exists as a real potentiality, the principal of a principality whose allure extends everywhere, stalking peoples' hearts, even the hearts of young children.

Looking back on it now, I realise that there was a palpable though not recognised kinship, between the sadism of Brady and Hindley, and the underlying groundswell of insatiable sexual indulgence that was forever being fetched up by the marketing of all sorts of erotica, that quickly caught the attentions of the growing minds and appetites of young children like myself. I no longer believe that these things merely siphoned off the sexual frustrations of unfulfilled adults. They did far more than that. They created obsession with sexual satisfaction, where only interest had been before, and incidentally created obsession with the satisfaction of appetites in general. They inflamed appetites rather than subdued them. And by enlarging and intensifying the realm of secret desires, they undermined the personal trust that glued families together. That secrecy created falterings, and the opening up of possibilities, that otherwise might have remained dormant long enough for love to gain a firmer foothold in the face of life's temptations and hardships.

I was not a pugnacious child. I'd been circumcised as a baby for medical reasons, and for reasons I will explain later, I'd been left with a deep-seated fearfulness that showed itself in moments of crisis. I felt familiar with death, felt that I knew it intimately, and felt that it knew me just as well. It never seemed a far off thing, but always something immediately present and dreadful. Because of this I over-reacted, and still do, when I was threatened by bullies or risky situations. Invariably I would be gripped by fear, to a degree that the choice between fight and flight was for me entirely notional. No matter what the circumstances, no matter how humiliating the consequences, when I was threatened by bullies I would flee. For some reason that I did not understand, I was weak and cowardly, and I loathed myself for it. However, I had to live, and although I loathed my cowardice, I loved my living flesh far more. As so many of us do then, I made excuses for myself, and portrayed myself to myself as someone who at least had redeeming qualities. I soothed my humiliated pride by reassuring myself that at least I wasn't afraid of climbing trees – well – not the one's I'd already climbed anyway. And as *I* saw myself, I was basically a good person, the fact that I frequently amused myself by teasing and testing my younger brother until he cried, presenting no impediment to this flattering self-assessment. I remember how shocked and bemused I felt, when once, a good-natured boy intervened to stop me vexing my brother in the rec' in this way – the 'rec' was our nickname for the local recreation ground that had football pitches and open areas to play in.

"It's OK – he's my brother," I remember saying.

"No it's not OK," the boy replied, "Stop it." I was dumbstruck. I think now that both my brother and I, owe that boy a lot. He helped bring me to my senses by sowing a seed of doubt and self-questioning. It still took many years to ripen, and is yielding fruit even now, but it produced benign changes from that very moment. I felt self-conscious and ashamed, and that is as it should be, for my behaviour was mean and abusive. Unfortunately, though ultimately for the good, my deepening sense of shame at my own abusiveness and weakness, had the immediate effect of consolidating my lack of self-confidence and self-worth, to which I responded by trying hard to cover it up with a more attractive persona. I self-consciously tried to become a better, more grown up person, whereas in my heart, I was more certain than ever that I was a hopelessly weak and immature one. More and more at school, I became the likeable wag, the joker of the group, cheerful and friendly. But those who knew me better, knew better. They knew that behind the act, I was miserable, and had a mean streak, just as my sports teacher came to realise that I was 'a bloody little liar', though why, was not something he was concerned to inquire into, so that his condemnation became one more reason to feel ashamed and hide behind my increasingly elaborate façade. I *had* lied to him actually. I had come up with some lame excuse for why I hadn't attended a swimming lesson at the local baths. It made me cry to be branded a liar by him, but I just couldn't face admitting the truth that in the life-saving classes we were having at the time, whenever I pretended to be the drowning man, I was so ticklish that when someone tried to 'save' me, I went into fits of laughter, and started gulping in so much water that I really was in danger of drowning. I knew if I tried to explain it to him, he'd just tell me to stop being silly, and make me carry on. On top of the fear of drowning, I didn't want to be laughed at by the other boys. It was humiliating, and I couldn't face being the object of everyone's derision. So I bunked off. The teacher really rubbed my nose in it, and could only see the lies. He never knew the real reason for my behaviour, and as far as I could tell, he didn't really want to. I think now he was just another bully like all the others.

By now, I was at grammar school – an all-boys school. The regime was quite tough, and you could expect to be caned if you stepped too far out of line. But the toughness of the regime was reflected in an equally tough hierarchy amongst the boys. In every year-group, certain individuals stood out as the natural alpha males, the ones who could take the worst the school could do to them. And they were the rulers when the teachers weren't there, which was most of the time. Somehow, you had to steer a path between the teachers and them, which involved some pretty dexterous footwork. The persona I created for myself, fitted into that strange double-headed community, in a way which was as perfectly adapted to it as I could make it.

This was a time when schoolboy jokes got dirtier and coarser. The bad boys seemed to see it as a proof of their hardness, that they could refer to women and girls as cows or cunts or slags or tarts. They pretended to feel nothing but contempt for the feminine sex, yet they all wanted to show that they were sexually experienced. And so it was, that at our local youth club, it became a matter of routine that as the evening went by, a conspiratorial air would thicken, before predictably, the lights went out, and the bad boys from the boy's school quickly groped some girl's breasts and legs before the lights came on again. One girl was quite mature for her age, and had the body of a woman, but being blessed with a large blunt nose and eyes that few girls coveted, she was more desperate for attention than most. One evening after the club had finished, she and her friend sauntered down a narrow lane that led to a ford in the stream behind an old carpet factory, and there was set upon by an excited gang, led by the boy's school bad boys. She yelped and squealed as their hands grabbed at her and scratched her as they felt beneath her undergarments for their sought after prize. Yet week after week she'd take that same walk followed by that same unruly pack of boys, and the same thing would happen each time. You'd have to be blind not to see that sex was a raging fury, that if they let it, drove people in pursuit of ecstasies of every kind, with no respect at all for love or kindness or decency. One thought of it as an ever present element, like the wind or the sea, that ran through the very substance of things, and affected all in one way or another. One thing I knew though, was that I hated the boys at school whose hardness expressed its pleasure in unjustly tormenting others weaker or simply gentler in temperament than themselves. Thankfully not all the hard boys were like that, and some would protect their friends from the worst excesses of the others. I remember one boy whose example filled me with awe. One day, someone older, who in truth had always seemed a decent sort, pulled rank on a group of us playing in the workings of an empty building site. But a boy playing with us was indomitable. He wouldn't give an inch to the older one, and so the older one twisted his arm until he began to cry. Satisfied, the older one set off to leave, but no sooner had he done so than the younger one picked up a stick and threw it at him. The older boy came back and twisted his arm some more until he cried again. Off he went again, and again the younger boy picked up a piece of tree root and threw it at him. The same thing happened a third time and a fourth, but the young boy never gave in, and the older one went off, not knowing how to get the better of him. How I wished that I had had the young one's courage.

Gradually then, as the years went by, the different emotional strata began to define themselves and extricate themselves from each other's orbits, where temperaments clashed or were headed in entirely different directions. When tackled by a bully head on, there wasn't much a coward like me could do to avoid some method of appeasement – most were satisfied if they made you cry – but they couldn't be there all the time, and as things inexorably drifted towards the practicalities of adult life, the concerns of parents and teachers seeped into our minds and behaviour as if by osmosis. And in truth the young blonde with the tight jumpers, pencil skirts, pointy breasts and lipstick, who helped run the youth club, was far more magnetising to the gentler souls like myself than the poor girl at the centre of the club's weekly impromptu orgies. Not that the helper's comparative wholesomeness dissuaded me from lusting grievously after her. Oh what I would have given to lift up that skirt and that pullover to feast my eyes on the delights concealed beneath. I daydreamed of it many times, and thought of her as pure sexual sweetness – a sweetness all the more desirable the more familiar I became with the barren emotional waste lands which the grammar school alphas inhabited.

2

Pornography is a kind of masturbation; it's a way of looking at things to give oneself sexual pleasure. That first time I lay in bed in the sunlight, my willy tingling as it felt the caress of the bed sheets, was an innocent and spontaneous thing. But what about the second time, and the third? Though I think I must allow as motive the need to understand the mystery of myself, and the actions I took to interrogate that mystery, in addition to that, there was another motive: the pleasure of anticipating pleasure. When the anticipation of pleasure took over from both revelation and interrogation, then at that point, masturbation began. When I dreamt of that woman in the wash basin, it was a sexual revelation. But what was it when I began trying to peep up my Mum's skirt? Or when I took the medical encyclopaedia out of the sideboard cupboard to look at the drawings of lactating breasts, or turned from the Grattan catalogue pages on children's toys and fishing tackle, to the pages on women's bras and girdles, was I merely probing the mystery of sexual desire, or looking pornographically at pictures of women? Does it matter from my own point of view that those images were not meant to be pornographic? I don't think so. Sinfulness comes from within, not from without, and I do think, no matter how scornfully the modern mind may mock the idea, that masturbation, no matter how innocent its beginnings may be, is ordered towards sin. There is much truth, I think, in the old saying, that masturbation makes you blind. For if one fails to grow out of it, it becomes a form of disordered desire, disordered because the masturbator either adopts an entirely narcissistic attitude dependent on physical self-stimulation alone to achieve erotic satisfaction, or, in addition to this, and by far the more common, arouses himself by contemplating an image of some person he desires, outside of any actual sexual relationship with that person – he simply uses her or him to achieve his own exclusive ends. Either way, he cheats his own sexual desire of the satisfaction it seeks, and violates the women or men, girls or boys, whose sexuality he steals by capturing their images for his own private use. If sexual love is the purpose and fulfilment of sexual desire, then masturbation is personal failure. It confines sexual desire to a solitary sterility for oneself, while turning a blind eye to the full reality of those whose sexuality one derives pleasure from.

But a boy cannot not be interested in sex. It is in his nature to be interested in it. If he tries to stop himself, he will only displace his interest elsewhere, either deeper down into the bedrock of his mind, or into some innocuous activity but with an unnatural and inappropriate degree of enthusiasm, that in lacking authenticity, only turns his life into a lie. And should the reader imagine that greater modesty on the part of adults might help alleviate the problem, I'd say yes I agree, but that it would not remove it entirely. For erotism does not always require an erotic image to awaken and sustain itself. After all, there was nothing intrinsically erotic about the bed sheets that wrapped themselves around me on that distant sunny morning. What *was* intrinsically erotic was my willy. And there is nothing anyone can do about that. In another avenue of sexual exploration, my lively unfettered imagination, inverted the polarity of sexual intercourse when I discovered that I enjoyed pushing things – usually old fashioned hair clips – into the hole in my willy. Some readers may be shocked at this, and consider it perverted, but be that as it may, unhampered in my privacy by others' opinions, I found it pleasurable and exciting. I had no idea why, and I had no idea that it might be considered perverted. For me it was just playful exploration.

I don't know at what age one is supposed to grow out of all this sort of thing, and realise that erotic pleasure is properly sexual and belongs in the context of a personal relationship. I suppose it should coincide with the moment one decisively leaves one's childhood behind and takes possession of the self that until then has belonged to one's parents. But there are very many factors that influence the timing of that moment. And for some, it never comes, but instead merely lingers on at the boundary between a perennial childishness and a half-hearted adulthood. Here one stands astride two distinctly different ways of life, never wholly letting go of childhood, while never wholly giving up the hope of growing up. In this state, one continually rebounds back and forth, and it is because of this, that the influence of social convention has such great moral significance.

In a society rapidly abandoning its traditions, social convention is a very complex thing. For the less weight tradition carries, the more weight is correspondingly carried by the opinions and behaviours of one's peers. And where tradition and popular opinion no longer see eye to eye, the individual must steer his own path between them. At the age of twelve, a great part of public opinion for me, meant the opinions of my mates, including Roger Blakely, who first unashamedly introduced me to grown-up masturbation. One day, out in the wood at the end of our streets' gardens, a group of us had been climbing trees and bird watching. But then Roger turned up, and as one elated by a wonderful new discovery, and wanting passionately to share it, he decided to show us slightly younger boys what happened when you masturbated. When he'd finished, and much to his amusement the inevitable had happened, we smiled rather sheepishly hoping to goodness he wouldn't want us to do it. Thankfully, some brazen girl friend of his acquaintance came along, and distracted him, but the relief proved short-lived when she offered to do the same to us as he'd done to himself. This was far too much for me. Even just her proposition, let alone the act proposed, I felt to be a sacrilegious trespass across the boundary of my self that I had only ever shared with loved ones. Just to hear her words made me burn with shame, as if merely to understand her intention made me somehow complicit in it. Feeling so uncomfortable, I declined, and pretty soon went home for tea. Nevertheless, the idea had been firmly implanted, and that evening, trying to be as quiet as I could when I hoped my brother who shared the same bedroom was asleep, I endeavoured to follow Roger's example. It took a long time, but despite stinging at the crucial moment, I felt it was well worth the effort. And so began a new and very long chapter – more a many-volumed book really – in my sexual life. From then on it was a case of putting two and two together. Clearly, sexy scenes at the cinema or on television, were meant for masturbation, and masturbation meant for them. This was a sexuality of voyeurism in one who could not have what he so wished for. It seemed to me that there could be no return to the sheer sexual frustration of the past. A genie had been let out of his bottle and would never be put back in. I would never again enjoy that happy-go-lucky street life that I had enjoyed as a younger child, but instead became more reticent and self-absorbed. I withdrew more deeply into myself, my fear of humiliation at the hands of bullies discouraging me from having girlfriends. The more beautiful and attractive a girl was, even when she took an interest in me, the less confidence I had. For I knew that others would be envious, and would show no mercy when they saw me with her. I had arrived at the early years of adolescence then, with a great passion for the feminine sex, but no hope of being loved by a real girlfriend. All I could do was wish and daydream. And that is what I did. My childish fascination with all things sexual and erotic, led for long, only to more of the same fascination, and I became locked into the habit of masturbation. Not that I was embarrassed about this in itself. In my own privacy, I felt no shame whatsoever about it, though I did still desperately wish that I could be with a real woman.

In these long years of frustration for the want of relationship, and seeking release through masturbation, I did things that I knew would get me into trouble if I got caught. On a few occasions, I used my body to model my mother's underwear, and stood looking at myself in the mirror. Despite outward appearances, I had no doubts as to my gender; I was thoroughly heterosexual and male. Neither, in their object, were my actions particularly narcissistic or fetishistic. The clothes were simply symbols of feminine sexuality, and I never lost the sense of that. I simply wanted to enflesh them, make what they symbolised seem more real. My behaviour led to an embarrassing moment though, when I forgot to put them back in the drawer, and left them in a neat pile on my Mum and Dad's bed. My Mum found them, and looked me in the eye as she asked me if I'd been wearing them.

"If you have and your Father finds out," she warned ominously, "he'll murder you!"

I lied with great conviction, and denied everything. I never did it again.

What came as a great surprise, was when I was looking on top of my Mum and Dad's wardrobe for the box that contained my toy speedboat, and instead found a copy of Parade, a popular men's magazine of the time. Compared to today's magazines, the contents were very tame, but to me, they were everything I might wish for. Years later, when in an argument I confronted my Dad with *my* discovery, and he realised that *his* secret had been exposed, he feigned what we both knew was an implausible innocence, insisting it had been an art magazine that he'd brought home to clean up after someone had maliciously defaced it. So that made the two of us liars. Like my mother, I was merciful in victory, and not wanting to humiliate him further, replaced his secret with our new one by allowing him to escape into his comforting fiction. Ah how I loved my Dad.

I began my story around 1957, to the strains of Burl Ives, Perry Como, Danny Kaye, Frank Sinatra and their like. But by now we have reached 1966. Kennedy has already been shot. The Beatles have begun to grow their hair, leaving behind their mop-tops and their collarless jackets. Cliff Richard still keeps making hit records, but the Rolling Stones, the Pretty Things, the Troggs, the Animals, the Kinks, the Who, and still the Hollies, capture better the new spirit of the times. The Beatles have already made Penny Lane and Eleanor Rigby, which the stiff-shirts in my class complain bitterly about because of what they call the flat notes. The Beach Boys' 'Good Vibrations' is just about to flood the airwaves, and fascination with psychedelia, is becoming a fashion essential. I am about to move far away from Yorkshire's West Riding, to the wild Northumbrian border country where England and Scotland meet, and to a mixed school seventeen miles away from my new home. And the next time I will see Michael Jarvis, who out of sheer spite, had torn a page out of my new stamp album the day after my Dad gave it to me for my birthday, will be at a pop festival where he will be wearing a black leather jacket, a brightly coloured bandanna around his now much longer hair, and signalling to me the love and peace sign. While I get over the surprise, I will share with him and my new friend Joe, the Japanese sake that my Uncle Larry gave me, and feel a glowing inner conviction that things are getting better, and something new is being born.

3

A change came over me when we moved to Northumberland, a very welcome one: I was granted the blessings of anonymity. Northumberland had been a second home to me. For many weeks of the year, every year of my life, I had stayed there with my maternal grandparents whose home it was. They lived on a country estate in a picturesque secluded cottage, their nearest neighbours being a gardener who worked for the estate, and a farming family whose farmhouse lay on the far side of an adjacent field. Apart from close relations then, and a few estate workers, I knew no one there socially, and no one knew me. Consequently, when I began my fourth year of secondary education at a new grammar school in a nearby Northumbrian market town, no one knew the history behind the persona of this apparently good-humoured boy with the strong Yorkshire accent. And that provided me with a spacious freedom to do things without being oppressed by the heavy cloud of apprehension that had previously hung over the doings of my life.

Also, in the company of girls, the boy's anxiety to prove their manhood, lacked the callous edge that it had had at my former school. Where at the boys school, girls had been the subject of much lurid speculation and fantasy, here girls were present in the flesh, to dispel the wilder myths and temper the worst excesses that could stem from them. Despite the equal involvement of girls in the school community, it was still the case that the boys and girls formed two distinct groups, and especially with the onset of puberty, individual behaviour was mediated by the separation into these. Boys and girls were able to define themselves as such, in relation to their opposite sex, which moderated to some extent, the intensity of competition within their own group. Boys were still boys of course, and sometimes slugged it out in playground fights, but their identity as boys did not stand and fall on their relationships with each other. It involved the girls too, and that meant the girls themselves had a say in the matter. A bully might feel the urge to puff himself up at some victim's expense, but if the girls chastised him for it, and made their disdain apparent in a way that only girls can, then both the bully and his victim were changed by it. The bully's ebullience was dampened, while his victim's demeanour was encouraged. If you could see that girls still liked you, in spite of your being bullied, then it wasn't the end of the world if you weren't an alpha male. And if, despite his prowess, the bully's brutality earned him rejection by the girls, then he gradually realised that he didn't hold all the winning cards. I realise now, that this only held for as long as the girls retained the feminine softness nurtured by their traditional upbringings. Alas, nowadays, that softness is no longer cultivated among Western girls as it used to be, due to an egalitarian shift in perception of what the feminine ideal should be. Now, girls seem almost as likely as boys, to be hard and vicious, ambitious and indifferent, lustful and abusive. Back then however, my heart was lifted by our move, and I began to meet girls again. Meanwhile, my own harrowing of my brother Graham's emotions began to subside, though he continued to suffer in my shadow, as my relationship with my father deteriorated into incessant guerrilla warfare – partly out of the natural rebellion needed to become my own person, and partly a consequence of beginning to see him as he really was, without the filter of childish idolisation.

I only began to realise just how badly Graham had suffered at my hands, when many years later he reminded me of it. The age difference between us, and the bad example of our father's impatience with us, had been a toxic combination for him. On the few occasions when our father would play with us, he'd angrily chastise Graham when seemingly inevitably he'd clumsily kick over the toy railway trucks or model houses we were playing with. It was only natural immaturity at fault, but our Dad, who I doubt had ever known much patience in his own childhood, made Graham feel that it was a very personal one, and at the same time reinforced my own resentment at having to suffer it. It was a scenario that in various ways was repeated over and over throughout his childhood, so that he lost any relish he may have had for physical activities or sports, and inclined instead towards game-play and fantasy.

For Graham, the nadir of his suffering came around the time he had just reached puberty and I was approaching the end of adolescence.

"Thee look after thy brother," my father had always said – I was his first-born, and he entrusted me with responsibility for his second.

And always our Mum's shrill voice shouting, "Will you two stop arguing," "Go out and play," "Be nice to each other!" had rung in our ears.

We'd always been 'we' to my Mum and Dad, and so Graham and I saw ourselves almost as extensions of one identity. But having been entrusted with so much responsibility for him, it went without saying that I was the dominant one while he was the malleable dependant, amenable to my wishes. That was the set up, with my short-tempered father at the top of this power structure, and my brother Graham at the bottom of it. So, even though I wasn't the least worthy of my Dad's trust, my position had ensured that I was favoured by him while my brother had felt a step removed and consequently more oriented towards our mother. In that way they'd developed a special bond between them that I'd sensed and resented. In response, I'd acted like a male animal defending his harem, and treated my brother as a contender ready to take what was mine, except that I'd used teasing, sarcasm and ridicule rather than antlers or teeth to demonstrate my superiority.

How I'd felt about Graham, then, had been a mess of emotions. Often we'd spent hours absorbed in fun and laughter, but at other times, inflamed by a jealousy I didn't understand while frustrated by his immaturity and seduced by my own greater power, I had imbibed an evil brew of vengeful and resentful feelings combined with the general impotence of my youth, and that human capacity for inventiveness which can be so wonderful and so wicked. Even as I'd loved him, I'd fallen into the habit of directing him in the joint venture of our brotherly fellowship in a manner inevitably biased by my own self-interest, something which he'd naturally accepted because of his love for me as his older brother. At the same time, being so much forced by circumstances into companionship with him, that companionship had held back my own natural maturation, until eventually even my beloved Grandmother had had to suggest that I was too old to be playing with the toy soldiers we'd so much enjoyed playing with. Being typical children, we'd kept naughty secrets, shared only between ourselves, which, despite my abusing of it, ever strengthened the exclusive bond between us. Now, as my conscience had belatedly begun to mature, making me feel ashamed of how rotten I'd behaved towards him, our sense of sharing a single profoundly intimate identity still lingered, and it was this bond – an otherwise good thing – that led us face to face with an evil that inhered in the bond itself, bringing us to the limit of its virtue.

There was no incestuous sexual attraction between Graham and me, just that bond, which proceeded more at my pace and for my convenience than his. Our parents had always shown irreproachable respect for the special privacy of theirs and our genitalia, and by example had passed that modesty on to us. But with adolescence, and my growing wish for independence and for possession of my own body, things began to change. With growing independence came growing freedom from habitual morality, and the need to establish a personal morality of one's own. This opened up a new arena in which everything could and had to be re-tested to assess its moral worth, and between ourselves, my peers and I re-tested much, especially the taboos that had been handed down to us in the form of simple, unquestionable prohibitions. Usually, especially in sexual matters, our natural modesty remained a guiding element in our explorations, but nevertheless, the social character of sexual attraction was now asserting itself more strongly than ever, and my friends and I joked and talked of sex all the time, sneaking looks at porn whenever we could, and ribbing each other about our chronic masturbation. So far, so normal. But on top of that, and providing the crucial background to it, was the revolutionary erotism of the new liberal individualism that was flowering in the aftermath of the social upheaval of two world wars and the constant rise of a confident materialism. Religion was being all but forgotten among the popular masses, and replaced by a liberalising rationalism. If one could find no rational reason not to pursue some desire or other, then one should pursue it – why not? There was no reason not to – no God – no sin – just rationally guided freedom. Even paedophiles would make headway in justifying their predilections in this liberal post-Freudian atmosphere with its acknowledgement of childhood sexuality, openly expressed in the Kids' Issue of Oz magazine which I subscribed to around that time. Needless to say, this new emphasis on rational justification magnified our generation's natural moral speculativeness more than usual. Ideas were abroad which swept over us with all the power of fashion, and being young, we were particularly prone to following the latest fashion. These were the sixties, and life had cast off the drab post-war austerity of the fifties to become sexy, colourful, and ever more masturbatory.

As I began making friends with people at my new school, I became aware of how much more than I, the boys were relaxed with each other about their awakening sexuality. It became known to me that one group who I liked, had gathered together in a friend's bedroom to look at men's magazines and masturbate. I was taken aback by their frankness and their familiarity with each other's sexually aroused bodies, and began to feel dissatisfied with my comparatively embarrassed self-consciousness. Other conversations and revelations increased this dissatisfaction whilst at the same time challenging my inhibitions. And the mood of the times, was that inhibitions were a hindrance in the way of free self-expression, with the implicit insinuation that inhibitions were a bad thing while free self-expression was a good one. Even homosexuality, which up until then we had reviled as something unnatural and disgusting, was becoming the object of sympathy in a way which went far beyond merely putting an end to its persecution. Rather, homoerotism as such, was coming to be seen as a valid expression of the individual persona, regardless of its precise roots in the person's biological or social history. Such influences so affected me, that whereas previously I'd simply been surreptitiously naughty without questioning the naughtiness of what I was doing, now, as time had gone by, it seemed that all my preconceptions and gut instincts as to what were right and wrong, what was natural and unnatural, had been sprung up in the air. It therefore seemed to me a tentative step towards personal freedom and liberation, when one evening, it occurred to me to suggest to Graham, that we try masturbating each other. The fact that I had always treated my poor brother who was nearly four years younger than me, as a convenient means to my own amusement, even to the extent of tormenting him to the point of anguished sobbing and wailing, and that in this latest suggestion I was still taking that selfish abusiveness for granted, was something that either escaped my awareness, or I subtly ignored. As I'd belatedly begun to mature, I'd begun to feel ashamed of how rotten I'd previously behaved towards Graham, and by now the affection I'd felt for him as my lifelong playmate, had begun to dominate over my petty egoism. But the taming of this chaotic tangle still left a confused and confusing mess, and it was in this mess that this new episode in our brotherly relationship was unfolding.

My sense of decency alone made me acutely aware of the thinness of the ice upon which I was now treading, but I had followed the lure into a sexually experimental frame of mind, and was now similarly luring him. Lust was present, certainly, but not for each other. Our common desire was merely to expand our sexualities more deeply into the realm of the real rather than remain semi-dormant in the background impotence of our wishful thinking. So we tentatively tried to act on it. But by then I was becoming a young man and he was still just a boy! – we both knew it! I wasn't like him anymore. I'd changed, but hadn't fully grasped how much or what it meant for us. Now the realisation of this broke the thread, turning Graham around first. It didn't feel right, he said, and he didn't want to go any further. Thus the balance between the forces at work in me was altered, and without his willing it too, there was nowhere to go with it. How far I would have gone had he not stopped it, I don't know. I would like to think, not far – but in any case, as far as we'd already gone was far enough – too far for Graham to avoid feeling himself despoiled. True children of Eve, and similarly blinded by our respective desires, we'd put innocent shame to one side and eaten of the forbidden fruit, only to find ourselves burdened by consequences of our fateful behaviour which we hadn't foreseen. For both of us, it was a decisive moment, though I hadn't realised then, just how long its reach would be. For Graham, it was a moment that seemed to sum up all that was dismal and abusive about our family life. It wasn't just that the 'sexual liberation' that my friends and I were so enamoured with, was too far beyond his years, but that in following my less than innocent lead as he usually had done in our brotherly union, he knew we'd crossed over into something new, something that was no longer just the idiotic bullying of a conscienceless sibling child, but something infinitely more malevolent, something truly wrong that went against the natural order of things to leave us marooned, cut off from the fountain of goodness that had always been ours, poised on the brink and already tainted by an irrevocable sense of disgrace that could not now be banished back to the unknown. However innocent our motives in themselves may have been to begin with, by narrowly following them we had transgressed the proper way of things and had come to know the very nature of what the Church calls 'sin'. Graham knew in his bones that we were betraying ourselves, and that I, his older brother, was betraying him. Innate shame alone could have protected us from our transgression, but as all growing children do in one way or another, we'd disobediently ventured far away from the secure certainties of home – and anyway, where would we be without that adventurousness? – still at home clutching our Mum's skirts? But with adventure came risk, and Graham now found himself in an evil place in which he sensed the incestuousness that the secretive intimacy of our time-honoured companionship had led us to, now that like most other teenage boys I'd morphed into something akin to a randy bullock but more satyric, with libido permeating my very spirit and seeking out every avenue of possible satisfaction like some lascivious liquid intelligence. He'd been thrown back on himself and in taking the lead from me had taken possession both of the situation and of himself, but it had left him bereft of the bulwark of his older brother's reassurance, making him feel isolated in the midst of his family, truly alone for the first time in his life, a prelude to my actually leaving home after which he would then have to bear the full weight of my mother's and father's imperfections on his own. On my part, I realised that we'd reached the limit of what we could properly share of ourselves, and was ready to accept this as it was my own maturation that had precipitated the separation. For Graham, however, the dawning of this knowledge had involved a step too far that had broached and wounded his innocence, and forced upon him an epiphanic glimpse of corruption, and his need to retreat into a solitary and frightening individuality that had snuck up on him unexpectedly from the quarter that, for all its trials, had always provided him with a sense of security. Now, that haven had been sullied, transformed into a rank and sordid place, necessitating the final separate leg of his own adolescent maturation in rebellion against a visage of repugnance that had assaulted him. Tormented by terrifying feelings of loneliness, inadequacy, and vulnerability that would plague him for long to come, it was the final disenchantment of Northumberland for him, and he left as soon as the opportunity arose, never to return except for family visits. Meanwhile, I moved forward into a more pronounced adulthood and forgot all about the incident.

As I now reflect back upon my careless exposure of my young brother to my burgeoning sexuality at that time of our imminent forced emotional parting, I struggle to overcome the wish to inject explanations too quickly, which is just my way of trying to escape the moment of contemplation of my responsibility for feelings and behaviour that now offend my estimation of myself as a basically good person. If I am a basically good person, I must somehow fit into that idea, the eventuality of a basically good person feeling so desperate as to want to mount someone's leg like a frustrated dog. For that was me – just wanting to fuck something – anything – the mud in the margins of a pond out in the fields – my still young Grandmother who I spied undressing as she prepared for bed – the milking machine nozzles that sucked on the dairy cows' teats! It sometimes seems that the interior workings of my imagination possessed no bounds – that I could only struggle to contain them from the outside with superimposed moral judgements while feeling compromised and weakened by my evident presence on both sides of the moral fence that divided the two. Now that I look back upon it, I see that this is the morass of feeling and emotion in which humanity must necessarily discover itself and yet by nature be called upon continually to rise above and master. But master for what end? Isn't that the mystery that drives all morality onwards in search of universal truth, even while our loins are lapped by tongues of passion, and our hearts gripped by vengeful desires? Yes it sometimes seems like that, but only sometimes. For something moral existed before the erection of that moral fence so easily burrowed under by personal and collective cults of secrecy, some force directed towards the moral good, working even in the depths of the primeval swamps that brought forth all that lives, and whose foetid waters still lie at our root bringing forth all that we are. Why, despite all the chaos of impulsive feeling, was I inhibited by a deeply felt reticence which always restrained me from the worst that I was capable of? Why was it that despite my flailing concupiscence, I could still recognise the beauty and wholesomeness of things – a faculty that worked within the chaos, bringing order and limit to it the more I began to understand my role in it, and which, despite my abusiveness, still retained my brother's confidence? Now, I feel shocked and guilt-ridden that too often I could have contemplated things too indecent and unworthy to want to describe, continuing the path that I had trodden many times before of recklessly following my curiosity and my lusts under the veil of secrecy and shared intimacy with others. I feel shocked because so often the sense of moral shame was either absent or not strong enough to dissuade me from making this choice. I sailed close to the wind, courting disaster, desperately trying to probe every obstacle to my getting as close as I could to what I wanted, namely, power and sex. Too often, only finding out at first hand why evil was evil would turn me back from some chosen pathway, when by then it was too late and harm had already been done. Why couldn't I foresee the guilt and shame I would feel when I later beheld the consequences of my actions – as I had felt with unbearable intensity after I'd once shot a perfectly beautiful frog at point blank range with an air rifle, just to see for myself what would happen? Why was my love of life so short-sighted, so inadequate, so immediately selfish? Why was my understanding so weak? Is this how it's meant to be? Are all of the world's victims of wanton destructiveness the necessary price of mankind's acquiring wisdom?

But isn't my feeling guilty later for not feeling guilty before, basically dishonest? Isn't it just a way of trying to manipulate my perception of things, to alleviate the difficulty I have now in accepting the simple fact, that most human morality can only be constructed from just such painful experience of one's own destructiveness - "Forgive them Father, for they know not what they do," - that the reason why the flesh must be torn, and the blood spilt, is because life is worth it? The truth is, that lost innocence knows, from the moment that it is lost, that there can never be any return to what it was. It can only hope to try to make amends through remorse, forgiveness, and wisdom. The *fact* is, that whatever my opinion now of how it came about, in this brotherly divorce of ours, the bright light of reality had held us both to account, and saved both Graham and myself from the limitless shadow-world of private lustful imagination in which evil unchallenged inevitably flourishes. This, I feel, is testimony to the fundamental goodness that ruled over our family life, handed down faithfully from generation to generation, so that just a few words uttered from my vulnerable young brother's mouth could invoke the strength of that rule and turn us back from a path to disaster. How I pity those less fortunate than us, whose families have not been so ruled. What chance have they, alone and unloved, against the temptations of pleasurable abusiveness that crucify one's own soul?

By the end of my fifth year at grammar school I was sixteen, one of the youngest in my class. I was still a boy but becoming a young man. The year was 1968, and it felt as if the world was on fire. That year both Robert Kennedy and Martin Luther King were shot. And all at once, along with all of my friends at school, I began to notice the news footage of Vietnam, as if for the first time. Previously, I had looked at it as a child spectator of an adult affair. Now, I saw it as a young adult, and therefore as my *own* affair. And what I saw, appalled me.

I find it interesting, that in this brief history of my obsession with Eros, at least as prominent in my memories of voyeuristic absorption, are those involving violence. Like many boys, I was drawn to horror stories, and when still a youngster, the image of Frankenstein's monster had been etched into my imagination. I often used to draw it in doodles when I was in a reflective mood. At nights, I'd sometimes scare myself with the thought that the monster might be in the wardrobe, and I would keep a close eye on the door to make sure I could see if it began to open. But this was all a game one played with oneself in pursuit of self-mastery. And it was in that spirit, that later I read horror stories. One that stands out in my memory from my fourth year, was one I borrowed from someone to read in class at the end of term. It was purported to be an account of the torture and execution of a heretic in the middle ages, though I have learned since that the similar execution of St Hippolytus took place long before in third century Rome. The unfortunate man had been pulled apart limb by limb by horses at the behest of his torturers. And as the limbs were being pulled out of their sockets, the taut flesh was slit open, and molten lead poured into the wounds. Yet even so, the stricken torso continued to live. I remember my breathing slowing almost to a standstill as I read this, and felt as if something dark and heavy had crept alongside my embodied soul. It was hard to shake off this intimate knowledge of such fleshly human suffering. It made me fearful of being alive. God forbid that such a thing should ever happen to me. And yet all my former understanding of what it meant to be a man, destined in all likelihood for soldiery of some sort, told me that it was just such fleshly suffering that I must be prepared to endure to earn my manhood. If my grandfather had lost half his stomach at Passchendaele in the First World War, and my great uncle James his lower jaw at the Somme, and if my uncle Edward had fought at D-Day, and my uncle Bill as a commando in secret missions to who knows where, why then, would any less be expected of me? All of us boys had some sense of this, and many of us already had a preference as to which of the armed forces we wanted to join if it came to it. So, obsession with the suffering of the flesh, was more than morbid curiosity. It had a real purpose. It allowed one to look the worst of death in the face, and still remain standing and unbowed. It was a ritual, in other words, that allowed initiation into the nobility and dignity of the human person, in the face of Nature's adversity.

But just because the possibility was offered, did not guarantee that one would pass the test. In the actual circumstances surrounding the Vietnam War, things became more complicated. After years of growing consternation at the continual stream of dead and gravely wounded being returned to grieving US relatives, and night after night of TV coverage showing the reality for the Vietnamese people, of massive American bombing, the deliberate destruction of the environment by spraying with toxic defoliants, and the havoc wreaked by infantry-led search and destroy missions, then, with the details becoming known, of the mass rape and murder by

American soldiers, of women and children at the village of My Lai, which, in the light of growing anecdotal evidence from returning war veterans seemed just the tip of the iceberg, a point came when even to many who had formerly supported the war, the way in which it was being fought appeared criminal from top to bottom, and seemed to make America, and by association the West in general, no better than her enemies. It wasn't just the indiscriminate horror of modern warfare that made this so traumatic for us, but the terrible sense of guilt and shame, that the West's political and military leaders could have considered the deliberate perpetration of such a moral abomination, an acceptable method of self-defence. There seemed only one way to redeem ourselves, and that was to bring the foul thing to an end as quickly as possible. In that febrile atmosphere, the scepticism towards war that had arisen in consequence of the cataclysm of the First World War, and towards the prospect of nuclear conflagration during the Cold War, resounded once again. Rather than the potentially ennobling character of war, what was emphasised instead by the footage of Vietnam, was the corrupting effect of its sheer depravity. And to myself and so many of my contemporaries back then, it seemed that war was a morally unacceptable obscenity that we must in good conscience absolutely oppose. Where that left my attitude towards my grandfather and my uncles, was a position of great respect, underlain with a perception of them as victims, as cannon fodder. War was not seen as the *outcome* of *political* failure; rather, it was seen as an *act* of *moral* failure. Thus scepticism towards politicians, generals and other establishment figures, was transformed into scepticism towards war per se, pure pacifism in other words.

Now the fact that this was a somewhat appealing stance to take, for someone like myself who remained uninitiated into manhood, was something made easier to overlook, as long as one retained the admiration of decent attractive young women. And since in fact opposition to the war was very fashionable and chic, a badge of honour for the new anti-heroes of the day like Jim Morrison, Jimi Hendrix, John Lennon and a host of other glamorous rock stars, it was very easy to be admired by young women if one followed one's anti-heroes' self-consciously rebellious example. Instead of competing in the hierarchy of the rut, we competed instead in the inverted hierarchy of anti-authoritarianism, subversion and self-immolation. To the opponents' opponents, their militant pacifism was nothing less than treachery, an action which threatened to leave their country defenceless against external aggression. For many of them, the more protesters burned themselves alive the better, and they'd be only too willing to help out with a handy box of matches. No one should underestimate today the depth of hostility between the two sides. The conflict was waged between those willing to accept this use of military violence as a means to defend their country against its enemies, and those who were not. That at least, was the long and the short of it for most of *my* contemporaries, who had little understanding of the political realities that had led to the war. The attempts to politically justify our anti-war stance, came after our gut reaction to the news footage and to the maturing depth of the rock music that so viscerally captured the pathos and anguish of the situation.

As I have said, the principle tactic of the anti-war movement was subversion. But it was a subversion that soon became far more than a mere tactic. For what ultimately was being subverted, was the kind of personality structure that could if necessary, tolerate, and indeed prosecute, war, though what exactly that meant, was the subject of a disagreement that belied the apparent unity of the anti-war movement. Given that toleration of war, is axiomatically the defining characteristic of the usually masculine warrior in all human societies, the summation of pacifist radicalism was a sustained uprooting from human consciousness, of *all* traditional gender identities, from the very primitive, to the very modern. To be more precise, what became the chief target of the movement's subversion, was what was regarded as the traditionally alienated character-structure of the human male, and the traditional gender relationships thought to be responsible for creating it. Initiation into warriorhood, is the traditional passage from boy into man, a passage previously honoured and upheld by all members of society regardless of gender. A movement was now begun, which sought to abandon and excoriate the traditional masculine personality across the entire social spectrum, seeing it as intrinsically evil and repressive. Whatever their claims to prior political precedents like the American Civil Rights movement, the British Suffragettes, or the general move in the West towards decriminalising homosexuality, it was the maturation in popular consciousness of this revolutionary belief in the malleability of human gender and its rightful freedom from repressive social control, that provided the ground for the radical feminism and gay liberationism we are familiar with today.

I first became consciously aware of gender politics, through the celebration of homosexuality, which itself belonged to the general celebration of erotism, in 'underground' newspapers and magazines produced by and for the youth culture centred on the anti-war movement. Although much of it was pacifistic, it would be misleading to characterise the anti-war movement as a *peace* movement, since a good number of its activists were neither peaceful nor pacifistic. Many were not anti-war as such, but anti-American, seeing the American state as a brutal aggressor in the service of American capitalism. These people were actually in favour of armed struggle by the Vietnamese communists, and wanted America to lose. Many linked the daily oppression of blacks in America, to the oppression of peasants in Vietnam and other parts of the world, and correspondingly made a link between their respective struggles for freedom. This sentiment was reflected in the underground press, and also inspired the boxer Muhammad Ali's refusal to be drafted into the US military. A paper called Frendz, was a very strong supporter of the IRA. And International Times as I recall, gave much support to Jerry Rubin's and Abbie Hoffman's yippies – radicalised hippies who did not reject violence as a means to bring about revolutionary change. Other papers leaned heavily towards pacifism, but all of them, no matter where they stood editorially, tried to contain the tension between pacifists and those who supported revolutionary violence. It was easy to swell their support while they focused on what they were against, an echo of which could be seen in the now regularly lauded million-strong march in London in 2003 against the impending military intervention in Iraq, which included many thousands of radical Islamists, defeatist socialists and anti-capitalists, alongside the pacifists, peace promoters, Little Englanders, and opportunistic journalists.

The underground papers were spectacular to look at, and clearly showed the influence of the movement's widespread use of hallucinogenic drugs – especially LSD, which was the strongest. If you haven't taken LSD, it is hard to imagine what its effects are like. One of the things it does, is intensify one's sense of colour to the point where it can become unbearable. The use of colour in the underground periodicals, was wild and experimental, visually stunning. Another of LSD's effects, was the distortion of ordinary processes of perception, so that things wouldn't appear as they normally do. Rain might suddenly appear as continuous thin lines descending from the sky. A sound might unexpectedly begin to reverberate, echoing into the distance and ending up in the imagination where it would mingle with hallucinatory reveries. Full blown hallucinations might appear, which could be wonderful or terrifying, beautiful or horrific. LSD was known as 'acid', and the experience associated with taking it, known as a 'trip'. Acid trippers were seen as heroic cosmonauts of inner space, and had a way of dealing with the extreme emotional possibilities thrown up by the drug. 'Let it all hang out', 'let the river flow', and 'stay cool', were all often used catch phrases which give some flavour of the attitude taken. According to the acid guru Timothy Leary who borrowed heavily from the Tibetan Book of the Dead, the trick was to not grasp at passing experiences. Whether they were good or bad, beautiful or terrible, they would all pass away if you let them. Instead of clinging to them, you should find your empty centre, and hang out there in the eye of the storm while the trip spun around you in all its riotous glory.

But what if you discovered that it wasn't the eye of the storm that was you, but that gory riotous glory? What then?

In all fairness to the acid-heads, they did warn of LSD's dangers. People did have bad trips from which they never recovered, ending up instead, either as residents of mental hospitals, or in need of long-term medication and therapy. And yes, some really did jump off high places thinking they could fly. But the hubris around LSD was in full sway, and one supposed that bad things only happened to someone else. I took LSD only once, when I was seventeen, and found it to be everything I'd read it was: incredibly powerful, incredibly beautiful, incredibly frightening, and lastingly disturbing. There were two things that I found particularly difficult to cope with. The first, was that apart from the frenzy of colour and psychedelia that roared through my mindscape, as if being projected onto the back of my eyelids independently of what my foreground awareness was attending to, there was an accompanying sense of being driven at full throttle with one's foot hard down to the floor. I hated that feeling, and felt abused by it. I felt I'd poisoned myself. The second, was a terrifying insight arising from a hallucination that I had. In my mind's eye, I saw a tall lean young man from a party the night before, standing before me wearing a bright lemon-yellow jacket. As he looked at me, he struck a match, and let it go out. Then, with the blackened end still smoking, he reached forward and touched my cheek with it. To my amazement, I actually felt my cheek burning intensely, and jumped up out of my chair shocked. What came home to me with terrible clarity, was that I could feel as real, anything I happened to think about. It wasn't just visual or auditory images that could be hallucinated, but physical feelings too. I wanted the whole thing to stop at that moment, but the effects of LSD last for many hours, and I still had six or seven to go. I retired to my bedroom, and clung tightly as if to a talisman, the signet ring my father's father had given me before he died. I prayed to him and I prayed to Christ, to watch over me until I'd come back to my senses. And just as people 'in the know' used to say, I didn't come back from my trip to the same place I'd embarked on it from. I had seen things that weren't easy to digest, and others that were entirely indigestible and could only be put behind me. Worst of all, I became susceptible to vague irrational fears, panic attacks, and a blanket of heavy deep depression – enough, all in all, to provide a lifetime of material for therapeutic inquiry and soul-searching – which in itself, I dare to opine, had no little value. Truth to tell, I was a failure as an acid tripper. I could not, and did not, want to let go of myself. Far from being an intrepid cosmonaut of inner space, my feet were firmly planted on the ground, if not positively rooted in the primeval swamps. Instead of flying in the spiritual ether free as a bird, I felt stretched all the way from the earth to the heavens, and unsurprisingly felt very very tense. Healing, for me, meant not, letting go, but rather, recapturing my God-given ground. And the real value of LSD, lay in its comprehensive illustration of how not to be – which included much of what I had taken for granted about myself, and about the youth culture at the time I took it. Ironically, in due course, LSD propelled me into the heart of the deepest and most painful truths of my life, and at the same time, out of the youth culture which had prompted me to take it.

To connect this to my train of thought, the youth culture that I had happily participated in, as well as containing a great moral motivation for spurning the traditional male psyche, was also bolstered in that direction by its experience of hallucinogens, which stimulated so-called 'non-attachment', or, to put it more commonly and more bluntly, carelessness, as a way of dealing with the inherent chaos of hallucinatory experience. If one denied any sense of natural propriety, then being rendered more or less dysfunctional by LSD, or by the much less powerful Cannabis, could become a source of amusement rather than of alarm or apprehension. And in that frame of mind, other people who were bothered or offended by one's strange or unconventional behaviour, were regarded as 'straights' and considered 'uptight', language and sentiments now more familiar in the gay scene. The fault was theirs, not yours. Thus the freedom so much vaunted by the youth culture, insofar as it sought to overturn and annihilate traditional values and social structures, was no more than a tyranny to those who recognised these things as expressions of a fundamental human reality. Farthest out on a limb in this direction, went Charles Manson and his adopted family of tripped-out hippies, who took it upon themselves to show the world the fearlessness of revolutionary freedom, by ritually slaughtering the pregnant actress Sharon Tate and her friends, in her Hollywood home. Of course, despite their hippy lifestyle and appearance, they were immediately disowned by the illuminati of the youth culture, who insisted they were exceptions who'd gone off the rails. But I don't think so. They were acid-heads, home-grown by the psychedelic drug culture, and only took to its honest conclusion, a direction implied by the abandonment of tradition and convention in favour of the existential purity of the empty centre. For what is nature if not convention? Take away convention, and all that is left is a vacuity capable of anything. I once believed in all of this, and so I hold up my hands and accept my share of the responsibility and guilt for the things that it led to – even the murders of Miss Tate and her friends. If only that were the end of it.

Political movements need common, even mythical, objectives around which to unite. Once American troops had left Vietnam, the youth culture was left without a common cause. Predictably then, the anti-war movement, already riven with divisions in an alternative hierarchy of revolutionism, soon fragmented, the divisions themselves dividing into an exotic array, including Trotskyists, Maoists, Stalinists, Marcusians, socialists, anarchists, ecologists, feminists, gay liberationists, and so on. And each sub-division divided further, amid the tensions felt between the struggle for doctrinal purity, and the wish to achieve practical results. Most of the groups that I have mentioned so far, leaned politically to the left, but the deep-seated individualism that typified the youth culture, could also become manifest in the anti-state attitudes of the radical right, soon to win power in the persons of Margaret Thatcher and Ronald Reagan.

What had appeared to be a unity had really been no more than an alliance of convenience with the different trends of thought coalescing around their common opposition to the war. As each trend sought to remould the individual mind in its own idealised image, they all cross-fertilised each other so that the movement became a cultural hot-house forcing the evolution of new personality types. The generation gap, already manifest in the 1950s and said by the radical artist Jeff Nuttall to have stemmed from the "bomb culture" that under the shadow of nuclear war made hay while the sun shone, grew wider and wider. Parents often complained that they no longer knew who their children were as they searched within themselves for clues that might help them understand behaviour they had never witnessed in their own youths. Large numbers of the young seemed full of contempt for everything that had already been built and achieved, and showed it continually by breaking things. They broke street lamps and telephone boxes, bus shelters and municipal playgrounds, derelict buildings and derelict people. And they did so with a sense of moral impunity that, as they got older and stronger, invariably grew so self-assured that it challenged not only the moral authority of the establishment but its physical power as well. In other words, they began to act as if they enjoyed immunity from the law and its agents, and as well as sowing some of the seeds that led to the policeman Keith Blakelock's butchering in 1985, became the godfathers of today's street gangs and volatile feral youth. Not long after I left West Yorkshire, a boy at the youth club I had belonged to was gashed across the throat with a broken bottle and killed. I knew the victim and I knew the killer. I had always known it was on the cards and only a matter of time before something like that happened. But the authorities were fighting a losing battle. Not Borstal, nor the cane, nor the slipper, nor friendly cajoling, nor pep talks, nor moral lectures either, were forceful enough, imaginative enough or confident enough, to match the scale or depth of the problem. It is too easy to say that tradition was being lost. More accurately what was happening was that the continuity, the living connection, between the old and the new, was being broken, leaving the young isolated and having to fend for themselves. And in that circumstance we behaved no better and no worse than you might expect. We reverted to the condition of people who have not yet become civilised and must still go through the labour pains of giving birth to such a state. That is why our culture contained such extremes and entertained so many and such diverse possibilities. The many ideas and ideals that we explored or embraced were ancient not new, but what *was* new was the extent of our alienation which gave so much fertile ground to these things.

Of course life went on and people discovered and rediscovered love as people do, and had children and became reconciled with parents and grandparents. But the reconciliations, the dropping back in of people who had formerly 'dropped out', did not return things back to normal. For the challenging of authority by those who had opposed the Vietnam War or who earlier had demonstrated their wish to 'ban the bomb', had effects that reached far beyond their own social milieus or their own times. Marxist thinking had already argued convincingly that human nature is a variable determined by the material conditions of existence, which included social relationships, particularly those of an economic nature. Therefore what could be conditioned, it seemed to them, could also be un-conditioned, especially in the midst of revolutionary events which overturned the social status quo. And though by the time of the Vietnam War the totalitarian character of Stalin's Soviet Union had left people in the West with little confidence in the ability of insurrectionist class struggle to purify the oppressed minds of the world's exploited people, the notion that human nature was essentially a social construct had, if anything, become even more widely accepted, and formed the corner stone not only of pacifism's assault on the traditional male psyche, but of the outlook of every would-be social engineer with a blueprint for a new improved social order. Those in the anti-war movement who believed in revolutionary violence focused their critiques on attitudes they identified as bourgeois and supportive of the system of economic exploitation. Many young radicals came to believe that the gestation of revolutionary consciousness required much time and commitment, neither of which was likely to be available in the acutely critical conditions of military insurrection. Without such a successful gestation, victorious insurrectionists would inevitably make their new world in the image of their old selves and render the whole struggle a tragic waste of sacrifice and suffering. So it was felt to be a matter of urgency that the job of social transformation was begun here and now by changing one's own self and sharing that change with others.

One of the first things to go was respect for traditional marriage, which was deemed to have been an authoritarian structure whose purpose was the suppression of individual freedom in the quest to control sexuality. The popularisation of this view was hugely facilitated by the mass production and distribution of the contraceptive pill, and the legalisation of abortion. With these in place, the fear of unwanted pregnancy more or less evaporated, leaving a clear field for the practical realisation of libertarian ideas on sexuality. What previously only the weak, the headstrong or the dedicated libertine might have done, now, without fear of pregnancy, everyone was able to do. And so very quickly it became the norm for young people, male or female, to indulge their sexual desires without much thought, if any, for marriage. Coupling was seen as something organic that would endure if the partners were right for each other, or collapse in due course if they weren't. The ability to let go of one's lover if either you or they wished to move on, was seen as a meritorious strength, while clinging to a relationship that had become dull or sexually unsatisfying was seen as a sign of weakness or dependency. And the notion of living a chaste life until one married appeared positively antiquated and risible.

This was the context in which began a sea change in attitudes towards homosexuality. For if sexual relationship was authenticated by the spontaneous arising of erotic feelings, then as long as homosexual relationships were based on genuine homoerotic feelings, they must be authentic and should be accepted as such. From this perspective, the idea of a naturally heterosexual norm unjustly oppressed homosexuals while, conversely, the struggle for liberalisation of attitudes towards homosexuality implicitly undermined the authority and character of traditional masculinity. Since the new revolutionism was bent on precisely this end it followed as night follows day that the movement would make common cause with 'gay' liberationism and present homosexuality as a perfectly valid expression of erotic desire. By the same token so too did it present other forms of erotism, including the pornography that depicted them, in a sympathetic light, even, in the most radical of apologetics, paedophilia. All that mattered was that erotic acts were entered into freely without coercion. The idea of corruption was thus rendered as obsolete as the idea of an authoritative natural norm, and in that way stubborn naivety delivered untold numbers of innocent lambs to the predatory wolves that roamed through the wastes of peoples' minds.

Now all of this I say from the vantage point of hindsight. But when I entered my lower and upper sixth years at grammar school, what confronted me then, or rather, what surrounded me as the ocean surrounds the fish that live in it, were the currents of behaviour that resulted from these shifts in moral understanding and attitude. All around me the world was transgressing the values of holy tradition, but no thunderbolts, no fire and brimstone, were crashing down from the heavenly heights. And it seemed so right to want to do what came by way of natural impulse. The moral taboos that had framed our parents' attitudes to sex seemed oppressive and unnatural to us, and so we discarded them, reinventing for ourselves new norms of sexual conduct. Buoyed up by the arrogant complacency of our youthful vigour, we confidently ignored our elders' advice and, high-minded or low-minded alike, we followed our noses into lives led by feeling and appetite. We *felt* that the Vietnam War was a terrible thing, and so we opposed it. We *felt* that sexual excitement was a good thing, and so we indulged it. We *felt* that dressing conventionally out of respect for others was a 'drag', and so we dressed as we pleased, claimed it as our right and pilloried those who disapproved for their intolerance and unimaginativeness. We were young. We were the future. We were irresistible. And through sheer tireless persistence we got our way. There and then the world became more colourful but less respectful, more sexual but less loving, more imbued with peaceful sentiments but less able to keep the peace. Voices warned us of our folly but what they said contradicted how we felt ourselves to be, and so we didn't listen. What did they know? The world had been run by their values and principles for long enough, and here we were, witnessing yet another savage war in a world dominated by corporate greed and political acquiescence. If the proof of the pudding was in the eating, the pudding was proving to be only a mix of failure and joylessness. So why listen to those warning voices? What did we have to lose? Why wait for enjoyment later when we could have it now? In that manner the bonds of love between the living were weakened, while the dead, the witnesses of past lessons both bitter and sweet, were, as GK Chesterton once put it, disenfranchised. But a culture based on feeling has a very short memory and very little breadth or depth. Governed by feeling, what the eye doesn't see, the heart doesn't grieve over. Then peoples' moral sensitivities become volatile and easily manipulated by what is presented to them through film, television and the newer media.

Even music can become a drug, transporting one outside oneself into the balmy waters of ecstatic bliss. Perhaps music has always possessed this power, but what has not always existed is the ability to procure it at the push of a button. In tribal societies people make music together according to the seasons of the year and the seasons of life. And the music is part of the identity of the culture and its people. In my years in the sixth form we were evolving a new culture internally bonded by its own music. It was a simple music which, notwithstanding its vocal harmonies, was predominated by the lone voice and by rhythm. It pulsated with the immediacy of life and was loud and insistent in its moral stridency, but its too narrow form never allowed it the patience or magnanimity to embrace the heart of a nation. A nation might embrace it, but never it the nation. For to do that you must surrender feeling to perception, and dare to care for people through the quiet uneventful times of life as well as through the emotional highs and lows that rock music is so good at expressing. Instead, rock music dwells in and on the present to the extent that if one makes it one's only music one becomes trapped in the present and typically seeks, as the music itself so amply demonstrates, to break out of this confinement through the satisfaction of ecstatic dissoluteness. For this reason, when I look back on my passion for rock music I recognise that it was a music of youth, a music of desire for the fulfilment of the body, full of indignation at the horrors of the world that called on us to make such great sacrifices. It was also our tribal music that secured our boundaries, a war dance that established territory and warned against intrusion. As a music of youth it should have been transient, but as a tribal music it sustained a culture just as conservative and determined to endure as any other. We were here to stay, and we weren't going to be compromised by the inconvenience of growing up. We had, then, to use the language of tantric Buddhism which here is very apt, entered into and magnified a mandala, a mandala that turned youth into an idol to be worshipped, a mandala which had the self-worship of youth at its centre and which consolidated itself around that worship, placing guards along its boundaries and expelling all from within who became disaffected with its character. But what did I know of that as I diligently read my copies of Ink and Oz every month while strains of Pink Floyd or Captain Beefheart filled my bedroom and escaped out into the garden where they mingled with birdsong and other village sounds?

4

Standing on the station platform at Dipton Bridge, I felt weary; not the pleasant kind of weariness you feel when you've been throwing hay bales up onto a farm trailer all day, but a different soul-draining kind. It was a lovingly kept station with hanging baskets and tubs edged with trailing lobelia and honey-scented alyssum. Bright blotchy pansies and pelargoniums filled the middles. They should have cheered me, as should the floppy leaves of the lime trees across the railway tracks, but they didn't. The pink of the pelargoniums was too vivid and jangled my nerves, aggravating a feeling of aloneness that was tainted with the clawing strain of desperation. I hadn't enjoyed the evening anyway. It had been disappointing. The people I'd met I hadn't known very well but had been drawn towards by an admiration of the kind of people I'd thought they were. I'd thought they were hip, cool, rebellious, sophisticated, but what struck me about them when I spent some time with them was that they still carried the marks of their well-to-do middle classness, and for all their pretensions of hippy classlessness my insignificance to them was obvious. They had a centre of gravity of their own which I had no relation to, and they laughed at things in a way that was unwholesome and affected, its aim being only to reassure themselves of their shared identity. I didn't share that identity with them and didn't want to. I found it strange and unattractive the more familiar I became with it. They were the kind of people among whom suicide or attempts at it possessed a certain kudos – a proof of the depth of one's sensitivity to the world. It gave depression a veneer of nobility instead of recognising it as collusion with one's own oppression. My own sensitivity came out more in the form of cowardice and a shameless will to live. It may not have been very romantic but I didn't see any virtue in drifting into oblivion with an empty aspirin bottle by my side or, alternatively, in being rudely awoken by a medical team busy pumping the contents out of my stomach. I was such a fighter in my own way that thoughts of suicide would never enter my mind. For the same reason these people made me feel morose. Their vacuousness seemed only to add to my sense of there being something dark just below the surface of my life that remained ever-present and inescapable, like suffocating quicksand.

As I looked across at the trees in search of anything that might lift the pall that lay across me, I saw only a thin skin of appearances that seemed too fragile to contain the unfathomable darkness that it barely concealed. Everything I looked at revealed this darkness – this consuming, all-absorbing, non-negotiable darkness. When I saw the flowers I saw the darkness. When I sensed the cool air I sensed the darkness. When I heard the track rails ringing as a distant train approached I heard the thunderous silence of the darkness. My heart shrank from it and I felt lost, beyond reach. Only this shrinking fear and my longing to return to the lightness of life gave me strength to keep turning my gaze away from it. At times like this I could not attend to anything for longer than a few seconds before being overtaken by the feeling of being sucked in and overwhelmed. I had to keep frenetically jumping from one thing to another to avoid becoming transfixed. Three weeks after having taken LSD this was my life now. Whenever anything reminded me of it my memories opened out to the experience itself and began to transform how I experienced the present. The pink of the pelargoniums was no longer the pink of pelargoniums nor even the unobstructed pinkness of pink itself – it was not so much 100% pink as 1000% pink – so pink it made me shudder with horror and want to crawl into some comfortably gloomy nook where I could shelter from it. The constant recurrence and anticipation of intensity, fear and panic made my head ache and I could feel the blood pulsing around my skull. When things got bad and I could feel myself slipping away into this chaos of feeling, I brought myself down to earth by talking out loud to myself, describing where I was or what I was doing. This exteriorisation of my inner experience made it more stable and gave me more control over it. It was less inclined to spin off on a tangent or inflate with a magnitude of its own. And I found that some things had such strong comforting associations for me that they too helped calm me down. From the beginning when the drug had first begun to affect me, I had found that drinking orange juice deeply soothed and reassured me. It bought me time and gave me hope that I might be able to outlast the onslaught. Clinging, as always, to this hope I got up from the platform bench as the train pulled in and boarded it to return home.

The village where I lived was and still is more a hamlet really. It had no shops, but was just a higgledy-piggle with three short terraces of stone-built houses, a Methodist chapel and a small farm. It lies in a shallow dip in the hillside that rises up from the southern bank of the South Tyne just east of the place where the river's course turns south away from its dominant easterly flow, towards its source in the northern Pennines near Alston. On a wild ridge to the north is the Roman Wall, built by the emperor Hadrian in the second century, and to the north of that lie thousands of acres of sprawling hill pasture and forest before more massive formations bulk up around the diagonal Scottish border. The border stretches between Berwick to the north-east, and the Solway over in the west just north of Carlisle. Between the village and Carlisle is the final slope down from the last of the Pennine fells towards the Irthing, a tributary of the larger River Eden which flows northwards to Carlisle along the fells' western edge from its catchments beyond Penrith and Appleby. The nearest town to the village is Tynburn, a mile and three quarters away, a hardy little town that then supported the surrounding community of hill farms, small coal mines and country estates. On the north bank of the Tyne the railway line between Newcastle and Carlisle is squeezed between the town and the river, and in those days, looping round in an arc over a low stone-built viaduct, a single-tracked branch line crossed the river and rose gently through the pastures until, more closely following the river valley, it climbed all the way to Alston where once, for a period, a small lead-mining industry had flourished. When still a girl my grandmother had held a position there as a maid. She'd hated it. Alston was set higher up in the fells than Tynburn, and the family she'd worked for lived higher still on one of the bleak slopes leading to Hartside Pass. She'd felt imprisoned there, entirely at the mercy of her employers' whims. The summit of the pass is a popular tourist spot now, a favourite of motorcyclists who meet on weekends at a café there where the grandeur of the view of the distant peaks of the Lake District and the great sweep across the length of the Eden valley towards Carlisle, the Solway Firth and the Scottish mountains beyond, unfailingly takes your breath away. Approaching from the west the road to Hartside crosses a swathe of soft lush farming country dotted with pretty Cumbrian villages. Approaching from the east, except perhaps on a sunny summer's day when still a melancholy spirit will linger there, even now in the comfort of the high-tech interiors of modern cars the landscape assaults you. It assaults not just your senses but your very soul. The sheer barrenness of its endless square miles of dry moorland grass afflicts and oppresses you. You don't just feel dwarfed by it – you feel intimidated, cowed, deflated. It mocks human light-heartedness and optimism. It's not easy to frolic in land like this, unless you're one of the black-faced fell lambs, and then only until your first winter when your wool has grown long and has matted into a mass of dreadlocks that can cheat the cold insistent rain- or snow-filled winds while you huddle behind windbreaks hungry and wanting to graze. The whitewashed farms here are far apart and are usually set in small valleys or dips where richer more nutritious grasses grow and the valley sides provide some shelter. When, during my childhood, we would cross over from Durham to Northumberland travelling to visit my grandparents, the further down the Tyne valley we drove the more farms we would see until eventually we'd reach Alston, and after that the villages of Slaggyford, Coanwood, and Stonehaugh. After that came the road over Redpath and finally down to Dryburnhaugh.

There were four country estates around Tynburn: Weaver's to the south-east, Bullforth due south, Stonehaugh upstream along the Tyne, and Dryburnhaugh covering the quadrant north of the river on the western side. My grandparents lived in a little cottage at Dryburnhaugh where my grandfather worked for the landowner as a woodsman. My parents rented an old labourers' cottage on the Stonehaugh estate. It had once housed two families, and to facilitate that arrangement it had two front doors, one at the foot of the stairs to provide access to the upper floor, and the other below them that gave entry to the ground. In terms of modernity, when my mother and father had secured the place it had represented a step backwards, for, having last owned a two bed-roomed thirties house in Yorkshire which had an indoor bathroom and toilet, we now had to make do once again with a partitioned bedroom, a bath in the kitchen and a toilet outdoors. But it seemed a small sacrifice to have had to make to be able to escape industrial Yorkshire with its yellow skies and its black foaming rivers.

Why here exactly? Because Stonehaugh had been the site of a prison camp for German soldiers during the war and afterwards for a couple of years. This was where my father had been stationed during his National Service and where he had met my mother before eventually marrying her in 1951 and returning with her to his home town Calderbridge in Yorkshire to earn a living among the factories there. He'd begun his working life as an apprentice fitter at

Fairfax, a local engineering works, but there was more money to be had just labouring in the booming woollen industry and so he left engineering and went to work for a dyer instead. There he stayed until we eventually left the area. As far back as I can remember he used to come home from work with reddish brown hands and a vinegary smell on his dark blue overalls. The reddish brown colour came from repeated staining by the industrial dyes, the vinegary smell from splashes of acetic acid which was used to bring the natural oils out of the wool before dying it. In West Yorkshire the underlying ground was free of limestone and so the streams and rivers ran with very soft water. It lathered easily making the area ideally suited to washing and dying wool. On the back of this opportunity, other manufacturing industries had arisen to spin the wool, then weave it into carpets and fabrics or knit it into garments of clothing. For the raw materials to be brought in and the finished products taken out to be sold, there had to be roads, railways and canals. And on these were needed lorries, railway engines, trucks and barges. Some were manufactured locally and some brought in, but all, as well as the factories themselves, needed to be maintained by fitters, mechanics, builders, engineers, surveyors, architects and so on. And behind these were the butchers, bakers, cooks, nurses, doctors, teachers, policemen, magistrates and priests, along with their shops, bakeries, kitchens, hospitals, schools, constabularies, courts and churches. With so much activity going on and so many relationships taking place, it was not just commodities that were being manufactured but more importantly, perhaps, an urban industrial culture sustained by a characteristic consciousness that was fitted to it. By this I do not mean that all of the people there were industrious or creative but rather that their behaviour was adjusted to the parameters of the environment they lived in. In fact this intense network of relationships formed so commanding a role in that environment that human minds inevitably dwelt in high degree upon human affairs so that the world of humanity rather than the world of nature became peoples' most formative influence. This produced a kind of arrogance: not so much a complete forgetfulness of Nature as of a feeling that people no longer stood beneath it, that man with his factories and machines was master now and nothing but man himself stood in his way. But in this view Nature was seen as just raw material, a resource to be drawn on when it suited man's purpose. Nature as a living thing, as properly man's paradisical home, was very remote here from most peoples' hearts or minds, though not from everyone's. Whilst thousands immersed themselves in soccer and supported the cities' teams or fought rivals on the club-grounds' terraces, some fished the polluted rivers for roach and whatever other species could survive. Others ventured up into the dales at weekends to bird-watch or just ramble through the open countryside. But after having come to know Northumberland, such vicarious pleasures could no longer satisfy my father. He wanted now to be closer to Nature and became increasingly impatient with the concerns of urbanity. He had experienced the vitalising vitality of rural life and knew now what he was bereft of. The tension couldn't last and didn't, but for many years to come he could see no way out and all that remained was to endure and make the best of things. Like many others he drove us out to beauty spots at weekends but because of the necessity of returning so soon this only made us more miserable and downcast. I found it easier just to stay at home where I could become absorbed in playing with my friends. And on reflection I realise that Calderbridge was not by any means void of Nature – I saw my first Yellow Hammer on the outskirts of Calderbridge, as well as all the usual varieties of garden birds. But I make these observations only to emphasise how life in Calderbridge could be enjoyable for us only insofar as we put to the back of our minds the enervating richness of being in close contact with a truly natural environment. Although man inhabited and made his mark on the land in Northumberland, he mostly worked *with* Nature rather than against her, so that man's activities and men themselves were naturalised by it. In the industrial towns and cities this was not the case. Here Nature was by-passed by man's activities. She did not directly shape them or penetrate man's being, and so people became unnatural. Excitable they may have been, but inspired by their fellow creatures? No, at least not in their daily activities. At best, communion with Nature could only be a leisure activity, a mere pastime incidental to the rest of their lives.

For my father, having tasted the richness of his Northumbrian idyll, this had no longer been enough, and for him the higher wages to be had in this heartland of modern industry hadn't been worth the sacrifice of the inspiration lost with every dull day of tedium spent at the dye works. For years he had soothed his pent up frustration by soaking up the lunchtime bonhomie of the bars at the Albion or the Crown, only to reduce my Mum to snivelling each time as she watched the fat congeal on the joints she'd cooked, and the vegetables stop steaming as they quickly cooled and became flaccid and wrinkly. Five minutes would turn into ten, and ten into thirty as she watched the clock, waiting for him to come home, in what became a predictable weekend ritual. Eventually, after two or three years of it, things came to a head when my father's frequent eruptions of frustrated indignation at my mother's complaints, at last turned into hopeless despair.

"How about you two?" he asked, as he turned to my brother and I. "Do you want me to go?" His packed suitcase stood at the kitchen door under the dartboard where the wallpaper was peppered with holes left by a year's worth of missed shots.

"Leave them alone," my mother had wailed. "Of course they don't want you to go!" I loved him so very much, but how could the thought not cross my mind that anything would be better than more of this?

He didn't go. My brother and I went into the sitting room and waited to see what would happen. Things calmed down. Nothing happened. I sighed and stared out of the window at the drab patch of waste land across the street. We were used to it by then. Weekends were like that. And yet perhaps for my Mum and Dad it had been something more – a warning of what might happen if things carried on for much longer as they were. If nothing else, a change of heart took place, and not long afterwards my Dad announced that he'd found a job on Teesside, and that we were going to move to Northumberland. We left after my fourteenth birthday. I'd felt that I was going to heaven.

Nowadays I still treasure my memories of the hope that the beauty of Northumberland instilled in my boyish heart, a hope that lifted my soul within my body so that even my footsteps felt lighter when I thought of it. Northumberland was my rural paradise to the industrial exile of

Calderbridge. In the Northumberland of my heart I could forget the cowardice, the fear, the humiliation and the darkness that I associated with the place that had both spawned me and been the heavy ground that my life had for so long been stuck in. Yet hope wished for is not hope realised. Northumberland had always inspired me with its wild beauty, but it could never be an escape from myself. Even in Northumberland it was the same body of memories that roamed the hills, fished the streams, and tried to forget yet did not forget who and what I had been until then. Northumberland couldn't renew me on its own. It needed my cooperation, my assent, my courage. There *was* cooperation, assent and courage, but there was also resistance, refusal and complacency.

Once we came to live there, Northumberland was no longer a heavenly abode that my heart longed for amid the busy hum-drum grime of Calderbridge. Instead, it now became a real place filled with real people as prosaic as those I'd lived among in Yorkshire. They were mostly simple working people, the most intelligent of whom were still profoundly involved in the practical necessities of life. As much as I admired and loved their practicality, it became more and more evident to me that I was not one of them. I was of a different stamp, and I didn't feel this just because I was a grammar school boy. Though my intelligence was certainly capable of practicality, I knew that it was much more than this. I felt I saw more into the depth of things than others, and was deeply though imperfectly romantic. In my first efforts to befriend local boys, I felt uncomfortably conscious of the quality of my intelligence which, compared to theirs, seemed to be filled with a feminine sensibility and self-regard. Once, when visiting the Tynburn cinema, I noticed that as I was becoming engrossed in the film I was watching with a group of new acquaintances, one of them was looking at me and laughing, making me feel self-conscious and uncomfortable. He'd seemed a friendly sort up until then, but I'd begun to discover that his appetite for life was far rougher than mine. He'd relate fights that he or his brothers and their friends had had on Saturday nights with town boys from Longtown or Dumfries across the Scottish border. He'd laugh when he spoke of chairs being used to batter foes at local dances or in hotel bars.

"He says he can take you," he said, leaning over the row of cinema seats in front of us to speak into a mate's ear while nodding towards me. I tried to laugh it off.

"No I didn't," I objected.

He laughed again mischievously.

"*Can* you take him?" he asked me.

"I don't know," I answered, irritatedly, trying hard to appear to be concentrating on the film. I knew he was trying to test me, but I wanted nothing to do with it. I found some way to wriggle out of it, and avoided him in future, sticking to my grammar school friends who seemed happy to just let me be. One, called Hugh, a Scottish boy from Ayrshire who'd lived in Carlisle before moving to a village close to the meeting of the North and South Tynes, had even given me a Christmas card, an act of outward friendship that has lasted ever since.

I felt a freedom in my schoolfriends' company, and felt with them that I could break away from the historical self that I had become through my relationships in Yorkshire. I no longer felt completely bound to that imprisoned persona anymore. This wasn't a dramatic leap into nobility and bravery, but was rather the arising of a small but much valued measure of fearlessness. I simply became significantly less afraid of being seen to be what I was: sensitive, fearful and idealistic. I no longer felt so ashamed at not being a tough guy. I just wasn't tough, and that was all there was to it. There was no point languishing in any more self-loathing over it. It wasn't that I belatedly began to love my *inner* self – I'd always loved that, as I think we all do. Rather, I began to love my outer self too – my crappy, cowardly, ignoble self – the one which Peter Hack later tried to hang by the jacket collar on a coat hook in a hotel cloakroom while our mutual friends pleaded with him to calm down. He'd thought I'd taken liberties with his girlfriend at a party, which wasn't quite true since, or at least so I'd been told, they'd split up by then, and anyway we hadn't really done anything as I'd only been put up to it by one of her friends to lift her spirits, and neither of our hearts had really been in it. In my newfound freedom from other's contempt for my weakness, I began to feel that for better or worse, it was me. It was all I was – and I loved myself no matter what other people thought about me. It is true that I still didn't love myself enough, but it was a turning point, the beginning of a conscious acceptance of myself.

The path of self-acceptance, however, is a dangerous one to tread. After all, what is lovable about sinfulness? And where is the line between weakness and abuse of others? It isn't a visible line. Where, for example, is the distinction between two people running away from danger, one a brave soldier, the other an abject coward? It isn't immediately obvious. You can't master a self you don't possess, but neither do you possess a self you can't master. All my life I have lacked both self-possession and self-mastery. In real danger I have always voided myself of self-possession and run away like a terrified rabbit. I have never been able, or willing even, to attempt to master terror. When present, it has always consumed me, leaving me completely alone in its grip. As I write this, I cannot help recalling the reliance of my parents on fear of punishment to effect discipline. I do not feel that they were necessarily wrong in this, only that I needed much more to be able daily to overcome the sense of being a failure, and the feeling of proximity to death that lay not far behind it. But this brings me to a question that always looms large in my life: why have I, seemingly more than others, been so suffused with the sense of inadequacy when in danger? For it is this awareness that has fuelled my imagination's rendering of so many fearful things. Why have I always felt so thoroughly empty of hope when what was needed was struggle? Why so certain of defeat and so uncertain of success? I ask these questions fervently because I know that that black seam of abandonment by courage has always lain behind all of the greater and lesser evils that I have perpetrated on others. Was it a similarly hideous well of fear in the 'Yorkshire Ripper' Peter Sutcliffe's soul, that he could only blot out of awareness by annihilating what reminded him of it – in his case women in their sexual dimension? What in God's name can it be that makes knowledge so utterly terrifying that you must rid yourself of it, no matter what you have to do to achieve this? And who can help? Who in their right mind would be willing to share your knowledge with you if it felt like this? Who could suffer it without becoming similarly afflicted? Isn't banishment and the victory of ignorance the only plausible answer?

These questions impinge upon one's mind and body, whether one has clearly articulated them for oneself or not. They flow like currents, both consciously and subconsciously, placing their stamp on all of your feelings and thoughts. There have always been moments in my life when the subject of these questions has come into view through lapses in my evasions and forgetfulness. And so often when they have done, I have remembered the habit of praying to God, a habit instilled in me every day at school during morning assembly, and at Sunday school to where I suspect my mother's enthusiasm at sending me had more to do with giving my father and her a brief respite from parenting than of any wish to make me a particularly religious person. And, of course, as was the norm at that time, we had gone to church too – St. James's– the seat of our Anglican parish. This had been one family routine in which my father had not taken part. He must have thought it a good influence for his sons at that stage of our lives, but he personally could not give himself over to it, and often scoffed with raised eyebrows when hearing of the vicar having visited to chat and enjoy my mother's tea or coffee.

"Tea an' pie in t' sky," he'd complain. And yet at some time it must have provoked greater hope and passion in him than he usually admitted, as I once found in an upstairs drawer along with an old pocket knife, a Rolls Razor, and various other bits and pieces, a slim blue New Testament, given to him when he'd joined the army. Some of its pages had been ripped out, and I could picture him overcome with anger whilst reading it, and violently ridding himself of the offending verses. Never having been one to turn the other cheek, and with a fierce, barely controllable sense of injustice, it was no great mystery as to why my father looked upon Christ's ministers with scorn. He thought they were hypocrites having long preached a gospel of peace and love before later playing a vital role in encouraging his father's generation to march off to the hellish mires of Flanders. I often heard my Grandad say, "Next time they should put all t' parsons an' politicians in a field an' let 'em feight it art among 'em sel's." His attitude had impressed itself upon my father, and through him, upon me too.

But here we now were in Northumberland with Calderbridge behind us, my past there relegated to memory, not forgotten but gone. Here, this paradise of lapwing and curlew, pheasant and grouse, hare, rabbit, deer, salmon, trout, minnows, silver birch, oak, beech, pine, spruce, larch, juniper, gorse, broom, the great expanses of heather that covered the moorland and fells, the wide ribbons of fern, bracken and willow herb that festooned the stream banks and woodsides, the swathes of deadnettle and meadowsweet that soaked up the dampness of soft permanently saturated ground, perfuming the warm air of spring and summer days with their unmistakable heady scents while all around was the hum of busy flying insects and the cooing of wood pigeons and the excitable chatter of sparrows and chaffinches – all of this, would press upon us like a salving balm to heal our wounds and soothe our weariness. So I hoped and felt, at least. I hadn't realised that what is not forgotten is never really gone. Northumberland was not my lasting saviour, nor could it have been, no matter how uplifting its benignity was. And with time, the matters that began to impinge on my mind and feelings were precisely those in which I experienced lack. For as well as a rustic idyll, I needed the food of intellect and community with others who were like me. Whilst I never lost my deep love of the Northumberland that had made me so happy as a child, my soul turned more and more towards my school milieu, and the beckoning future that it was the gateway to. Rather more than the desire for academic success, what most motivated me was the idealism that perennially seems to assume so large a part in young people's lives. A cultural avalanche of music, poetry, literature and personal ethics was crashing over us, carrying away many like myself to wherever it would take us. It took me to art college in Bristol, before moving deeper into the South West peninsula where I joined a college friend in Devon in the city of Exeter.

5

Already in the early spring of 1971, I knew that I was not going to do well in my maths and physics exams. My only hope of proceeding any further with my education lay in art. I applied to colleges in Bristol, Leicester and Bath for a foundation course as a preliminary to studying for a Diploma in Art and Design which was the standard at that time. In due course, the letters fell onto the doormat inviting me to attend interviews, which I looked forward to excitedly. My Mum and Dad bought me a portfolio to gather examples of my work in. My father was sceptical of the venture, but proud nonetheless. He'd rather I'd applied myself to something more sensible and remunerative like accountancy, but at least this was something.

"Dun't thee end up workin' i' overalls!" he'd warn. I understood his concern, but I couldn't square it with my love for not only him but for my grandfathers too, and all of my uncles by either blood or adoption. That they'd all worked manually was an inseparable part of what I'd loved about them. My father's wish for my betterment ironically set me apart from him and his world, in a way that hurt me.

I idealised becoming a gardener like my Mum's Dad, or a farmer like Harroldson, my godfather.

The interviews at Bath and Bristol were on consecutive days, so it was arranged that I would stay at a hotel overnight to allow me to attend both interviews in one trip. The college at Bath was actually in the nearby village of Corsham. My recollection of it is of an old manor house or hall of some kind, and the tenor of the place seemed very traditional. The lecturers who interviewed me reminded me of my school art teacher, and were impressed with a pencil drawing that I'd done of the railway track up the line from our village, and the tall conifers that reared up beside it from the embankment's steep decline down to the burn below. The impression the lecturers made on me was austere and rather forbidding. In comparison, the college at Bristol, which I visited the following day, seemed more agreeably adventurous, and more to my liking. But what I remember most of these two visits is their location on either side of what happened in between them, a descent of my experience from mere lack of confidence in myself, to a state of panicked anxiety centred on an inexplicable sense of foreboding and an implacable dread of being alone. After I had checked in at the hotel in Chippenham, the nearest small town to Corsham, I had felt myself so overwhelmed by an unbearable sense of isolation that I could not bear to be still but felt driven to traipse around the town for hours until I was weary enough to rest. Though I am sure that much of this was the residue of my dally with LSD the previous summer, thinking back on it now, its precedents went farther back than that and restored to my consciousness the feeling of another occasion away from home when, at the age of twelve, I had visited Switzerland on a school trip, and felt myself similarly isolated in a hotel room full of school mates in the pilgrimage town of Einsiedeln. On that occasion too, I had been shaken by how unbearable the feeling had been, and had had to leave the dining table with the excuse that I needed to use the toilet. I had longed for the familiarity of my home and the comforting ambience of my Mum's and Dad's presence that I knew could shelter me from this stark abysmal feeling. After composing myself by rehearsing small but familiar elements in my manner of being myself, I again had to constantly keep distracting myself with activity to deflect my awareness from the feeling's terrible intensity. On both occasions, my distractions eventually succeeded in defusing the feeling, allowing me to gladly put it out of my mind. What I remember of it now is only a shadow of what it originally was, sufficient merely to recount it to others. For its trajectory still terrifies me as much now as it did then, even though I know I should follow it to its end to be free of it.

All of the art colleges offered me places, including Leicester which I felt to be too oriented to commercial design and advertising. I accepted the place at Bristol and went there the following summer.

Things I remember about Bristol: dope; the Doors' 'Riders on the Storm'; Quicksilver Messenger Service – especially the guitar solo on 'Fresh Air'; long streamers of recording tape that Richard, a housemate, had hung from the ceiling around his bed to make it feel like a four-poster; the old gent on the ground floor of the house we rented, who coughed and wheezed a lot, and always called me Chas, even though that isn't my name; Harry from Hull, who painted big slick realistic images of naked fleshy women; Denny, who wasn't just there but was always there *with* you, emotionally and intellectually, in the scary stuff as well as the funny; the hippies next door, who were so over the top they tied a bed frame between a skylight and their top floor stairs bannister, so they could crawl up onto the roof and drop unannounced into our place, bent on delighting us with their camaraderie – one of them, who had some teeth missing, extolled the virtue of his having stitched his longjohns into his trousers – what with his point of entry, his state of mind and his personal hygiene, he was high in every way; Lynne's boyfriend Dick, with his big u-shaped monkey smile and twinkly eyes – he was a painting student in the second year on the Diploma course who enjoyed our company and laughed a lot, both at us and with us – he once drunkenly but sincerely shook his head looking at Richard and me, and said, "You two are real heads!" – such affectionate flattering celebration of the atmosphere we were confecting, filled our house with gaiety and mirth; Denny's older brother Roland, who'd previously taken some improvised cocktail of DIY highs and ended up with foamy white stuff coming out of his nose, and a damaged brain – he'd grin emptily and generally act as if he only partly inhabited the world the rest of us lived in, correspondingly giving it only part of his attention as the invisible side of his life unfolded somewhere else while Denny resignedly looked out for him, worried for his safety and frequently encouraging him to go home to their parents.

I stood on the platform at Carlisle station with my packed suitcase and my portfolio at my side. My hair was longish and the clothes that I wore, all still paid for by my parents, were casual and arty rather than sporty. I never felt comfortable with the rugby shirt thing that many of my school friends had got into – it just reminded me of rugby, concussion and headaches! As I said goodbye to my parents, my Mum pulled me towards her to give me a tight hug, upsetting my balance slightly.

"Be careful," she remonstrated. "We'll see you when you come home for Christmas." Of course in those days, amazing though it must seem to young people now, there were no mobile phones! In fact at that time my Mum and Dad, relieved as they were to have gotten out of the urban mainstream, didn't even have a house phone. So there was no, "Oh I'll call you when I get there," banter. No, then when you were leaving you really were leaving. It was a truly uncertain parting in which you knew that until you saw each other again or received a letter, you could not immediately be sure of each other's welfare. All you could do was trust that everything was alright. These were mostly one-sided concerns just then, as my parents were still young and I was the vulnerable one entering on my first test of independent life.

"Look after thyself," my Dad said. "And keep thy nose clean!" He laughed exasperatedly, knowing his words were probably falling on deaf ears. He hid his real fears and as always made light of our parting. He just stood there, straight-backed like a man. And I began clambering onto the train – glad to be his but glad too to be getting out from under his rule. They stood there until the train began moving off, my Mum's face a mixture of sorrow and pride.

We waved and smiled, their figures slowly diminishing until I couldn't make them out anymore as the train rolled out of the station and on its way.

As I looked around the carriage and allowed the minutes to pass while the landscape outside changed from Carlisle's red brick and stone to the soft greens of Cumbria, I felt apprehensive. I was worried that I might again be afflicted with the sense of desolation that had come over me when I'd gone for my interviews. So far I felt OK, but I couldn't pretend that I wasn't concerned. Outside, the rich pastures were replaced by blanched brown moorland grass as we crossed Shap Fell to the east of the Lake District and headed down into Lancashire. As time went by I forgot to be concerned anymore and settled into the journey, my mind switching, as minds do, between passing thoughts, passing sights and sensations, and passing appetites. As we travelled through Lancashire towards the industrial arteries that connected Liverpool, Manchester and the West Yorkshire conurbation, the knowledge that we would pass by undeflected was not just gratifying but something that seemed to epitomise my experience of trains. To me they've always symbolised both liberation and liberty, and have always proclaimed it in the most exciting, grand and colourful ways, right from when I was little and clamoured to be picked up so that I could see the steam engines passing beneath railway bridges we were walking over, making everything smell of the sooty smuts and steamy smoke spume that escaped their funnels in great throaty puffs. I smiled as I remembered my childish delight and realised that I still felt it even now. The 'tiddlydik, tiddlydik' of the carriage wheels, reminded me of the countless times that the diesel between Newcastle and

Carlisle had passed along the line at the far side of the field next to my Grandma's cottage, making the rails sing like lullabies that soothed our passage into sleep. It was a pleasant way to be leaving Northumberland behind, and brought with it some of the perfume of my happiness there. I thought of my friends Joe, Hugh and Clem, and wondered when we'd meet again. And I wondered who I was going to meet in Bristol. No trace of doubt troubled me in this respect. It did not occur to me that I may not be proceeding towards the life that I wanted to live, or that it would not be peopled with dear friends whose company I could not be more satisfied with, and whose ideals would be my own. In this, my confidence was as impregnable as my naivety, and I am thankful for the protective veil thrown over me by it. Could youth ever find the courage to set out into the unknown if it did not enjoy the buoyancy of naïve hope? Now that I had set out into a future of my own, I felt a pang of hunger for what each moment would bring – until, like my earlier concerns, this also subsided as time engulfed it and I sat, occasionally jostled by the unevenness of the tracks, content to just be there.

It took four hours or so to get to Bristol's Temple Mead station. Then I had to find my way to the lodgings that we'd arranged through the college administrators. I was to stay in a room rented out by a young couple who, when I now recollect them, remind me uncomfortably of Fred and Rosemary West. Apart from having similar accents, the husband was a muscly labourer-looking type with tight curly not quite ginger hair and a broad snub nose. His wife was brunette with straight hair and glasses, but probably taller than Rosemary West. It's horrible how people like the Wests leave their corrosive mark on the world, making it a more suspicious place. The couple I'd stayed with had always seemed friendly and nice, the husband unreserved in his confident hard-working masculinity, his wife modest and dutiful, attentive to her husband's needs. I'd shared a room with another lodger, a young Welshman of my age who oddly, perhaps, left me with the abiding memory of his confession of vulnerability to delirium when suffering from flu. Not surprising, then, that he reminded me of a former Welsh acquaintance in Northumberland, an elderly dust-cart driver I'd worked with, who seemed to relish inveigling me with stories of Welsh miners dying miserably of what he called 'black heart', by which I suppose he meant pneumoconiosis caused by breathing in coal dust. To be honest, far from eliciting awed sympathy, because his proffered dark reflections were presented like credentials, he irritated me intensely, so that I'd want to defend my worldliness by saying, "Yeah, we've got that in Yorkshire too. 'Cause of all the coal mines there!" I don't think I stayed in the digs for more than a week – maybe the Welshman got the flu?! – I'm kidding. No, as soon as I began attending college I very quickly met a chap staying somewhere that was more roomy, and whose landlady was a cheery old soul well-known in the local pubs, and more than happy to allow someone else to stay in her house. That too didn't last long, however, for I soon became friends with Denny and Richard, and together with Lynne and Harry we rented all but the ground floor of a house together, where we stayed until we had completed our foundation year. The house was part of a terrace on a steep little street off Hotwell Road below Clifton, just before the main roads converge and wind alongside the River Avon where it flows through the deep gorge beneath Brunel's landmark bridge. The art college at Bower Ashton was on the other side of the river in the parklands of the Ashton Court estate.

Harry had had a room on Hotwell Road itself, overlooking the wharfs on the river. Before he'd moved in with us we'd often visited his place and got stoned and drunk together while listening to music. We'd often capped it off by strolling around the quays to an all-night café whose dark slabs of bread pudding were famed, justifiably or not, as the local dredger captain's favourite. I suppose our behaviour must have been tolerable for we were never refused or turned away. I read in an angling magazine not long ago that the fishing's good here now – as it is in the docks around London.

It was at Harry's that I first played John Lennon's 'Imagine', an album that preserved some of the stark candour and rawness of his earlier primal album, though with more utopian socialist pretensions. The latter was made whilst Lennon was immersed in primal therapy which he had been undergoing with Arthur Janov of Los Angeles. It was pretty much John Lennon, in primal pain, set to music. If you could bear to hear it, it was harrowing but profoundly beautiful and moving. At the time, I didn't really know much about primal therapy. I'd seen a TV documentary about it when still in the sixth form at school, and had Lennon's album. But that was about it. It was just instinct that drew me to it. As it had to Captain Beefheart's raucous music. I was attracted to the way in which music allowed you to feel what you otherwise might not be able to – like a Red Indian war dance perhaps, or the way the melodic themes and textures of more modern romantic kinds of music can so powerfully take hold of your heart and wring feelings from it that you weren't aware were there.

These early days of meetings and newly formed friendships were happy and invigorating. We danced a lot, drank a lot, and smoked an awful lot of dope, though I'm told most of it was far milder then compared to what is typically to be had today. Personally, I wouldn't know. I never touch the stuff now, and haven't for many years. But I fear my contemporaries are rather too inclined towards selectively rosy memories of our previous drug experiences. I'm sure that dope had a cumulative effect that eventually took its toll, certainly on Denny and me in Exeter a year later, probably affecting me more than him.

In the daytime in Bristol, we went to the college and, when not in our studio spaces struggling to be artists, we attended classes pertaining to different kinds of art. Some of my peers seemed to find their niche very quickly. Denny oriented towards sculpture, Richard towards film, and Harry to where he had been all along – painting. But I found it very difficult. It wasn't that I couldn't paint or draw. I just couldn't locate myself properly in the artistic scheme of things, and floundered about without any direction. I think now that I might have fared better in what had seemed to be the more traditional environment of Corsham; the openness of Bower-Ashton just seemed to dissipate my artistic energies. And what made it even more confusing was that as well as having a natural musical talent that had never been much cultivated, I was also a literary person and had long been a frequent visitor of

Ultima Thule's in Newcastle, one of the new wave of bookshops that fed into the burgeoning youth culture, exploring its literary and historical roots and its many influences in mysticism and political theory. Alongside Stevenson and Melville, the small bookshelf in my brother's and my bedroom in Northumberland had soon filled with volumes by Herman Hesse, William Burroughs, Jack Kerouac, Jeff Nuttall, Edwin Brock, Lawrence Ferlinghetti, Charles Bukowski. I suppose now I'd have to describe my inspiration as a kind of mystical romanticism, which I had not the faintest idea how to express in my own visual art. Part of the problem, I think, was that none of my tutors understood me, and therefore didn't know how or when to try to help me, though I don't blame them as I think at that time I would have been very hard to help. One of them was inclined towards a very painterly kind of art, so I spent many long hours trying to paint in a very painterly way, but without infusing any real soul into it. At school I'd spontaneously adopted symbolism as a means of communication, but here none of the tutors seemed interested. Yet one girl – Helen – produced wonderful little assemblages of exotic objects – beautiful feathers and silks and things – that she framed behind Perspex in varnished wooden cases. They were evocatively romantic with a mystique that fired up the imagination, reflecting an experience of sumptuousness that I had never had. I felt terribly proletarian and dull in comparison, and I began to lose confidence in myself as an artist. Not only that, but I began to notice an anti-intellectualism in the tutors which I didn't share and didn't respect. In that reaction, I was beginning to find my direction at last, but it wasn't towards anywhere that *they* could point me. Ironically, when it was really too late to pull any coals out of the fire, I forgot to be directionless anymore and painted some quite subtle monotone studies of light and shade under the studio's multiple light sources. The tutors were impressed, but it really was too late. My body of work was too eclectic, too poorly developed and too slim to impress any of my interviewers for the Diploma course. I didn't get in anywhere and faced having to return back to Northumberland with my Mum and Dad – a dismal thought.

As for girls, well, nothing happened. I wasn't ready. I wasn't confident enough sexually to be who or what I really was. Girls who seemed to fancy me had been too nervous and introverted, too vigorous and elemental, or just from too elevated a class background for me to feel able to identify with. I'd found them interesting, likeable, and often fun to be with, but no sparks had magically flashed between us to set alight flames of love, which was something I had known before and still longed for once again, something unique and personal that made us more than just hungry animals fighting for a place in the sexual pecking order. I found many of the girls attractive, but the only one with whom I hoped the attraction might lead to something was also not ready, and deeply distrustful of men's sexual attentions. She was too beautiful, I think, and had always found herself the object of male avarice and lust rather than love and affection. Now she didn't trust men's advances and played a very cool game. I liked her and found her very sweet. But I was just a harmless friend to her, someone she felt safe with, harmless because of my lack of strong focus, my malleability. It was fitting, then, that apart from my habitual masturbation, I lived out my year at college committed to a sort of chastity.

When my Mum and Dad came to pick me up at the end of the final term, they were shocked at how filthy the house was. They didn't say much but they were glad to get me out of the place. I took with me Denny's address so that I could keep in touch with him. He'd gotten into Exeter where I hoped to visit him.

6

Exeter. It isn't hard to conjure up the essence. Like most provincial towns, it had its share of modern concrete blocks, their ground floors used as shops or supermarkets dazzlingly illuminated by fluorescent strip lights. The special offers stood out just as brashly there as anywhere else. If you'd squinted through their flat expanses of glass you'd have recognised the same household names that you would have anywhere else, and perhaps have felt it was all rather nondescript. But if you had you'd have been forgetting the terrace of alms houses in St. Leonards, whose thick rust-red walls, smoothed off at the corners by hundreds of years of exposure to cold, damp and heat, looked as though they had been there always and should be allowed to remain for as long as Nature would permit. You'd be forgetting the once handsome iron bridge which led out to the north, its now flaking struts flanking an old factory with Buddleia sprouting from its dishevelled masonry. Behind it was a Victorian terrace, and behind that a grove of sycamore, ash and yew trees which overhung the no longer used cemetery in which they stood, and the monumental henge-like gateways to some catacombs which at some late point in history had been dug into the foundations of the old city wall. It was possible, if you were slim enough, to squeeze past the hinges of the barred iron gates, and walk upon the sandy floor alongside the vaults. In the musty dungeon atmosphere, as you peered into the dark shadows while sensing the dampness emanating from the sand beneath your feet, you would be inclined to wonder whether human debris still lay there motionless and pristine in the cold sepulchral voids set out before you.

On a summer's day, disturbed only by the occasional fumbling pensioner, dog leash in hand, you could lay back upon one of the gravestones that jutted out like ship's bows from the steep grassy slope below the catacombs. A breeze may have lightly flicked up wisps of hair so that they floated at right angles to your head. As you lay there prostrate, your eyes would be able to follow the skyward reach of the tree limbs which would sway slightly, like monks absorbed in meditation, and through the murmuring gaps in the panoply of leaves you might see, suspended in the blue infinity above, a shimmering floss of cloud. The cloud could be seen from a cabin that stood high up a valley side behind the city, its timber walls soaked in creosote, and its gabled roof overlain with blistering layers of felt and bitumen. It overlooked the Exe valley and the estuary contained within it. Beyond the estuary the English Channel began opening out to the Atlantic, and on clear days the sea's unsettled surface would sparkle as a myriad of tiny suns, each entombed in a watery prism, shone out with a cold wet glare. Sea frets would scoop out the sails of dinghies as their tidy hulls skipped hither and thither across the waves like the playful offspring of some intelligent marine creature.

Sea gulls would flock in turbid clusters over the mudflats at the river mouth and further inland over freshly ploughed fields. They would mingle with pigeons in hotel car parks and cobbled courtyards, and on the crowded green next to Exeter's cathedral. The cathedral's sand coloured hand-dressed stones ascended abruptly and rose high above the surrounding ancient cloisters. There, their surfaces abandoned the profound simplicity with which their upward lunge began, and instead assumed a rich and intricately carved variety of decorative forms. Presiding over these extravagantly laboured works, the battlements loomed, menacing and hawkish.

You'd be forgetting too the jewellers shop at the bottom of Stepcot Hill, its Tudor walls embossed with a latticework of dark oak beams, its tiled roof as steep as Matterhorn slopes; and the Maritime Museum with its cornucopic collection of small sea-faring vessels, some decked out in all their sail cloth finery and gaily painted, whilst others wallowed heavily, their black pitch-soaked carcasses compressing against the unyielding wharf the tractor tyres slung buffer-like across them.

Then there were the ever-present drunken sots who reeked of cider, and tottered red-faced about the streets or sprawled across park benches in bleary-eyed stupors, their brown quart bottles at their feet. There but for the grace of God . . .

I travelled to Exeter by coach on a bright sunny day at the beginning of October. Denny had written to me with his address, which I now found quite easily not too far from where the coach had stopped. Having spent the summer wielding a sickle to trim the coarse grasses that were encroaching upon the almost hidden saplings of a vast conifer plantation situated among the forest areas in Cumbria and Northumberland to the north-west of Gilsland, I had managed to save a little travelling money. It would do until I signed on and found myself a job of some sort. Denny was renting a ground floor flat in a large Edwardian house off Magdalen Road on the eastern side of the city. He quickly came to the door in response to my knocking, and when he saw me his bearded face lit up with a smile and his eyes creased and twinkled.

"Nice to see you man! Come in." He led me to the kitchen where he offered me a coffee.

"Yes please," I answered. "How you doin'?"

"Great," he replied.

"How's this place?" I asked.

"Yeah, it's OK – for now anyway."

"And the college?"

"That's OK too," he said. "Don't know many people yet, but the tutors seem alright. Yvonne's here though, and Phillip."

"Phillip?! Hah!"

Yvonne had been a fellow student at Bristol and, like Harry, was a painter of sleek nudes rendered larger than life on massive canvases. She was tall, fleshy and sexy in a Sandra Bullock kind of way, which frankly made it puzzling as to why she was with Phillip, a usually drunken alcoholic with a silly red boozy face, skinny trunk and limbs, and fair curly hair. He was a betting man, and when not in the pub would be in William Hill's backing horses.

"How is he?" I inquired.

"The same. Off his head most of the time!"

I smiled.

"A friend of Lynne's is here too – Wendy."

"Oh yeah? What's she like?"

"Different to Lynne. She's quieter and thinks more. Her work's different. More sensitive I'd say."

I nodded, hastily passing over my own still painful sense of artistic failure.

"OK, so where shall I sleep?" I asked.

"Couch do for now?"

"Sure."

"But there may be a place coming up soon we could share with some other people. I've arranged to meet them tonight."

"Who are they then?"

"A girl called Jeanie, and her friend Gwen. Are you hungry?"

"I could eat," I replied.

Denny began rummaging around one of the cupboards and took out a packet of red lentils and a handful of vegetables.

"How d'you meet them?" I asked.

"Jeanie's at the college and doesn't live far from here. Gwen's staying with her."

He put the lentils in a saucepan, covered them with water from the tap, then placed the pan on the lit kitchen gas hob to cook. Sitting down at a small table where the afternoon sun was shining through a side window onto the battered wooden surface, he pulled a crumpled plastic bag towards him, took out some cigarette papers and began to join them together. Then he broke the filters off a couple of cigarettes, split the cigarettes open and poured the loosed tobacco out onto the joined papers. Unwrapping a small green block of cannabis resin, he reached for a lighter and began searing the resin in the flame until it softened and gave off its characteristic pungent aroma. He crumbled small pieces off the edge of the block, and sprinkled them over the tobacco before finishing the thing off with a card tip ripped from the papers packet. Then, rolling the papers round to form a large cigarette, he licked the gum to seal it and twisted the end to keep the contents in place. He lit it and took a deep drag before passing it to me.

Like other forms of smoking, I think the paraphernalia and ritual of rolling joints was half the fascination of the thing. In a similar manner, my mother's father had cultivated a ritual around his pipe, slicing thin strips from his resinous bars of Warhorse which he'd rub down into shaggy fibrous wads that he'd carefully pack into his pipe bowl. And when he finally lit it, the aroma was as much a part of the ritual as the effect of the nicotine, filling the room like incense. Whereas my father's manufactured cigarettes had always given off a dry smoke that gave me headaches and feelings of nausea, my grandad's pipe tobacco smelled wonderful and complemented the entire atmosphere of the cottage with its mixture of cooking smells, potted pelargoniums and wood smoke from the fire. I remember my Grandma saying wistfully in a quiet moment many years later, "I like a man who smokes a pipe."

But smoking dope, like imbibing alcohol, was a very much more sociable practice in which people's different responses to the intoxication played off each other. Like all social rituals, it created a shared identity which offered reassurance, affection and humour. And these affected the quality of the intoxication, even when you smoked alone, since the solitary ritual still invoked the spirit of the social identity that had begotten it.

Denny and I laughed at each other as the drug began to take effect and our heads started to feel light and become filled with a rush of wayward thoughts, images, and pleasurable sensations.
"Phewph!" I gasped. "Haven't had any of this for a while."
Denny just laughed again and started chopping up an onion. Soon our eyes were stinging and welling up with tears.
"Jeez, what a couple of miserable fuckers!" Denny lamented.
Now I began laughing again and started to chop up a carrot. We became quiet and absorbed in the culinary task we'd silently assumed for ourselves. Eventually the meal was ready and we ate.

After I'd unpacked some things and cleaned myself up, Denny said, "We should be going."
"Okeydokey," I responded. "Ready when you are."
So we grabbed our jackets and left. We'd often played darts in the college bar in Bristol, and at the pub Denny now took me to, we once more indulged in the pastime. In Exeter, people drank locally made cider as often as beer, and our favourite in this pub would be a dry cider made in nearby Somerset. Sun and cider go uniquely together. It's as if the sunlight that ripened the apples has entered the drink itself and shines upon you from within when you drink it. It soothes and gently warms your senses, warming you not only to yourself but to those around you too. Unfortunately,

the acid from the apples gives you gut-rot if you drink too much, and makes your farts smell unpleasantly eggy! There always seems to be a price to pay for short-cut happiness! Back then we were still young, however, and shrugged off such inconveniences with the assuredness of youthful invincibility.

"You'll be sorry," sang Denny, mimicking a hollow-eyed doom-mongering cow's skull from an old Popeye cartoon as I began to down my second pint.

"Yeah, yeah, yeah," I replied dismissively. "Aren't they supposed to be here by now?"

"They are actually," he agreed. "But we're not going anywhere. Are we?"

"Nah. I'm happy here. Fancy another game?"

"You go first."

I launched a dart at the board, trying for a double twelve or a six. Then the pub door opened and the two women walked in, their faces smiling in recognition when they saw Denny.

"Hello Den," one of them said, the taller of the two.

"Hi," Denny replied, and repeated it as he turned to the shorter one. "This is Ced," he went on, and addressing me said, "This is Jeanie." He gestured towards the taller woman. "And this is Gwen." His eyes fell upon the other.

"Hello," they said amiably.

"Hi," I returned. "What would you like?"

"Oh," Gwen chirped with a note of polite surprise, "I'd like a cider please." She smiled.

"Could I have a lager?" asked Jeanie. "Thank you."

I turned towards the bar to attract the barman's attention and placed the order. Presently, he put the filled glasses down in front of me and I reached across to pay him.

Picking them up I strode towards the darts area and nodding at the board asked, "Shall we start again?"
"Yeah," everyone agreed, thanking me for the drinks.

As the evening unfolded and our darts games became punctuated with the joviality and laughter of our young adulthoods fabricating the enduring personalities that over the years would continue to express more or less the character of each one's particular intelligence and temperament, the differences between these two women began to shape my attitudes towards them. While Jeanie's life steadily flowed through her like a lowland river, reflective, sombre, and in its fluid depth forbidding even, Gwen was more spritely and vivacious, with a quick wit and humour. Gwen's natural appeal captivated me and I soon could feel an intensity tightening inside my chest, a pleasant quickening of the nerves at the centre of my body. It made me want to interact with her, not just by playing darts, which was fun, but through our conversation, which was in part investigative, but also revelatory and performative. In wanting to know what music she liked, and what authors, I laid bare something of my own intellect and interests. What would be the point of making such inquiries if the answers would mean nothing to me? And so she learned that I enjoyed music and books too. Whereas *my* musical taste leant towards the treatment of sound as sculptural form and texture, hers was more lyrical. I liked Beefheart, Pink Floyd, Yoko Ono, Soft Machine; she liked Van Morrison, Bob Dylan, Velvet Underground, tastes which she shared with Jeanie. Denny notably brought the Doors into the mix.

Gwen's openness would allow her to enjoy the shocking raw novelty of Beefheart's excursions into staccato phrasings of guitar and voice, interlaced with the bird-like warblings of his clarinet, and successive showers of drumbeats, marimba and xylophone notes that momentarily would constellate themselves in a particular ephemeral pattern before moving on to the next, as if produced by successive turns of some exotic audiophonic kaleidoscope. For Jeanie, in contrast, it was too much of a shock. As poetry, she mocked it for its seeming crudity. She couldn't bring herself to reach beyond the refinement of her beloved lyricism. She stumbled over the novel form of it, unable to recognise Beefheart as a quintessential emissary of American romanticism, a humorous portrayer of the immense American landscape and the human and animal characters who lived in it. While the Stones were self-confessed fans of the heroic American project, who, in emulating its adherents became adherents themselves and carved out new trans-national frontiers of their own, Beefheart, or Don van Vliet, as was his family name, was an original, a physical and spiritual son of America, a backwoodsman, a desert dweller, a mountain man, an Indian-lover. If British rock music grew out of the African experience of the European colonisation of America and the blues music that came out of that experience, Beefheart's music embodied the pioneer's experience of America, in which Navaho and rattlesnakes, medicine men and moonshiners, southern belles, negro mamas, weary bent-backed cotton pickers, bellowing smoke-belching steam engines, fiddle-playing homesteaders, beat poets and bohemian hippies, all had an honoured place.

As well as having an open mind, Gwen was good at darts.

"Shit!" I moaned, congratulating her as her dart point struck home in the double twenty to finish the game. She laughed as she walked back from the board pleased with herself. She was wearing a skirt of russet corduroy that flattered her trim waist and behind and swept down to her ankles. On top, under a short brown cardigan, she had on a cream blouse with a dainty floral print. Her fine hair was a mousey colour and did not grow very thickly, which accentuated the size and shape of her skull, reminding me occasionally later of a young child. On her feet she wore flat suede shoes. We played a few more games before giving the board over to someone else. Then Denny bought another round and we found a corner table to sit at.

"So what's this place you've found Den?" Jeanie asked.

"It's a house down on the other side of the river," he replied. "Western Road?"

"Oh yes, I know it," said Jeanie. "How many bedrooms?"

"Three. Four at a stretch. Are you interested?"

"I'm OK where I am actually, but you're interested aren't you Gwen?" She turned towards her.

"Yeah?" Denny quizzed, turning towards her too.

"Yeah," she confirmed enthusiastically.

"I was thinking of going to see it tomorrow night," he added. "Can you make it?"

"Yeah," she responded again, her eyes widening with excitement.

"Great," he declared.

"And you?" Gwen asked me.

"I'm on Den's couch at the moment," I explained.

And so the following evening we met at the house, Denny having borrowed the keys from the agent representing the owner. On entering, we wandered from room to room and generally agreed that it was reasonably clean, with more than enough room for our needs.

"Shall we then?" asked Denny, looking at us with his familiar twinkly eyes.

"Yeah," I answered.

"Yeah, let's," added Gwen.

Having made the decision to embark on this beginning, we each felt satisfied with ourselves, and strolling back down the road the way we'd come we went into a pub by the river to mark the occasion with a celebratory drink. The pub, the Royal Oak, would become our local in the coming months, and had a typical Devonian character with an old-fashioned skittle alley at the rear of the building. The whole of this plaything – the aisle as well as the balls and skittles – was hewn from wood, now faded and worn with years of use.

A few days later, our first full day in the house while Denny was at college, I felt sufficiently confident to take hold of Gwen's hand in a bid to solicit a favourable response. I'm not sure now whether she would actually have initiated it herself, and was just won over by my insistent optimism, but in any case I succeeded in establishing a reciprocal sexual bond, albeit a somewhat confused and faltering one. It was a damp autumnal afternoon shrouded in gloom, which made the warm glow of the front room gas fire's ceramic radiators – our only illumination as we let the light fade – seem comforting and homely. We'd finished unpacking most of our things and, having together set up Gwen's stereo player, had now begun to share our musical tastes with each other. Gwen played Tim Buckley to me, and I was enthralled. I had never heard anything like the vocal on 'Strange Feeling.' The lyric says, "I don't know what it is but it won't let go," and for me that's been true ever since, of the song as well as of its subject. The soaring cadences of Buckley's voice, pellucidly underlain by the gentle rhythmic support of vibraphone, double bass and jazz guitar, lifts my spirit above its too often stultifying absorption in daily affairs, to a realm of the heart in which what matters above all is the purity of love and one's fidelity to one's true self in its relation to others. Unlike a theological or philosophical tract, Buckley's lyrics did not try to explain what love was, or even declare it as so many popular love songs do, but examined and expressed its essence musically through song. His voice became more than just a part in a musical composition, or a speaker of poetry. Rather, like a jazz singer, he would break free from a song's preconceived melodic form to accentuate and personalise the feeling that was its true meaning. The idiom in which he did this, however, was not jazz but a loosely defined jazz-flavoured amalgam of American folk and rock, that was entirely and uniquely his own.

"That's fantastic," I sighed, shaking my head.

"Yeah, it is," Gwen agreed. "You must listen to Van Morrison too. And the Velvets."

She was kneeling on the mat in front of the fire and pulled the cardboard box containing her records closer to her. She rifled through the sleeves and pulled one out. Then she reached behind her, lifted the Tim Buckley disc off the player's turntable, and put the new one on, carefully dropping the arm and stylus onto the spinning vinyl. We spent the afternoon listening to record after record until we were weary of music. On my part, I was like a courting bird, trying to impress a desired mate with gifts, and in the heady atmosphere of the room's dimness, the weight of sexual desire bore down heavily. At the very least Gwen was agreeably amused by me, and eventually we touched and caressed each other. But unexpectedly, we fumbled awkwardly and painfully to unite with each other. It was the first time I'd been able to unrestrainedly be with a woman like this, and I felt a tinge of disappointment at the inelegance and imperfection of it. Without realising it, I felt a longing for my school girlfriend Kath Clement's measured but generous sexuality. That night I came to Gwen's bed and she laughed at my presumptuousness but didn't turn me away. In the weeks and months that followed, our sex became more proficient and the bond between us grew stronger, but always an insecurity nagged at me. Were we together now – boyfriend and girlfriend? I suppose it would be true to say that I wanted to feel we had conquered the separation between us and were now as one, each other's. But I sensed that only I was doing any conquering and that she was just indulging me. Though we came to each other's beds we retained our separate rooms. People would see us as being together, and she'd happily go along with that, but between ourselves I felt there was something lacking, an element of uncertainty that made me feel anxious – missing words, absent gestures, which made Gwen's freedom feel threatening. At the beginning, however, these were just seedlings of doubt which I shrugged off as my own faults. And as they grew I continued blaming myself in this vein. For now, though, we threw ourselves into life and, along with Denny, enjoyed our new house and our new and old friendships. We lived as a group and included Denny in everything we did, except in the bed. It just happened naturally like that. It was what we wanted.

7

The dole money was OK and I was grateful for it, but I wanted – I needed – a job. One day the Labour Exchange set something up for me out in the countryside. I was to go to a farm off the Sidmouth road just beyond Clyst St Mary.
"You need to be there by eight," the clerk said. An unlit pipe lay on his blotting pad on the counter beside a pot full of ballpoints and pencils.
"Thanks," I said. He smiled benignly, but with a trace of scepticism showing.

The following morning I clambered out of bed at six, hurriedly dressed and had cereal, then left. The busyness of the morning was already underway and the number of vehicles on the road was increasing moment by moment, each engine contributing to the general background hum. The air was still fresh from the cool of the night, and the sun was already rising above the horizon and up into a clear sky. That's how I began an unforgettable day tasked with reducing a foot of chicken droppings down to floor level in one of the farm's outbuildings. The droppings were stratified in compressed layers, tough as leather. The farmer had provided me with a fork, a mattock, a shovel, and a heavy old wheelbarrow made heavier by a thick coating of rust. It took an enormous amount of effort just to get the fork to penetrate the piled up dusty mass, and when it did I couldn't lever out any of the muck without the prongs bending. When I tried using the mattock instead, striking the fibrous surface with all my might, it just bounced off with no visible effect. When eventually I managed to gouge out a hole in the uppermost layer with the pick side of the mattock, I found it just as difficult to widen the hole as it had been to make it in the first place. After half an hour the first blisters were appearing on my hands, and after a further half hour they'd all burst, so that exposed raw flesh now pressed against the gritty rust on the tool handles and wept. The only way forward was through sheer persistence and painful toil, with very meagre results.

At midday the farmer came to see how I was getting on.
"I thought you'd be further," he observed disappointedly.
"It's matted and set dry," I replied. "It doesn't want to budge."
He couldn't complain much, and he knew it. The amount he'd agreed to pay me was little more than a boy's wage, and if the job had been going to be an easy one he'd have probably tackled it himself.
"Never mind," he went on. "You'm tryin'. You take your break now and be back in an hour. There's a pub up the road there. Good pahsties. The landlady makes 'em 'erself."
True enough, the pasty I had with a pint of ale was the best I'd ever tasted – full of lean beef, with onions, potatoes and swede. I returned on the hour as agreed, and set-to once again at shifting the obstacle. By the time the day was

finished I'd broken the back of it, but I still hadn't been able to clear around the edges. The farmer returned, and though less than magnanimous in his praise, nevertheless paid me what we'd agreed and let me go.
"Do you need me tomorrow?" I asked – more out of politeness than anticipation.
"Oh that'll be alright thanks," he replied.
I nodded, and walked off out of the farmyard, satisfied that I'd worked as hard as I could, but wishing I'd been able to make more of an impression on him. It hadn't been blisters and aching bones he'd been paying for, but results. But what more could I have done, I wondered. The stuff should have been soaked the night before to soften it. Then it would have been workable. I looked at my blistered palms and fingers as I walked along the lane between the hedgerows. They burned with a hot salty sting, but they weren't my first blisters. I ignored them and trudged wearily to the bus stop, feeling potent after having worked so hard.

I'd been stoned for days. The sky was heavy and grey, and I was sitting on a park bench with my back to a shrubbery, its dark green laurels mounting up behind my head. Above me, the leafless branches of oak and elm trees reached over to form a natural bower. I felt calm but tense. Gwen and I had been together for three months now and I was unhappy with the lines of stress that seemed to direct all of the emotions she provoked in me. I supposedly believed that love should be freely given, yet when put to the test I fell prey to a jealous anxiety, as when she'd visited an old friend whose Latin looks seemed to me far more attractive than mine. I felt inferior and that somehow she'd mistaken me for someone I wasn't. But it was a feeling I struggled against. It didn't fit in with the image I had of the person I wanted to be. Jealousy had no place in that image, and so I felt I had a particular problem. Why was I so prone to jealousy? I didn't realise how deeply I had been remotely affected by minds that were informing the youthful milieu I belonged to. It hadn't occurred to me yet to seriously ask myself why I thought jealousy was a problem, or why sexual freedom should necessarily be regarded as a good.

I gazed out across the park from my shadowy bower, watching a group of young teenagers playing football. My neck felt stiff and the beginnings of a headache were troubling me. I closed my eyes to rest them, and in my mind's eye saw Gwen, happy and enthusiastic as she gaily went about her involvements with people, apparently untroubled by the kinds of feelings that troubled me. Part of me felt happy for her, and part of me felt worried and irritated. Why was *she* never anxious? Why was it always just me? Did she just not care enough to feel anxious? It was a question I wanted an answer to but couldn't even bring myself to openly acknowledge.

And so while the boys in the distance exulted in their strenuous athletic efforts and fancy footwork, my thoughts moved back and forth between self-recrimination and distrust of Gwen. My feelings went one way and my mind another, but mostly I blamed myself and tended to settle on that position, just as I had been inclined to find fault in myself for having reacted badly to taking LSD three years earlier. Why couldn't I let go and just let things happen? Why did I feel I so badly needed to stay in control? The questions seem ridiculous to me now, but *then* I couldn't see past them.

Sitting there, I remembered an occasion when my friend Joe and I had been returning from a festival in Reading and had slept on an old schoolmate's floor in High Wycombe. I'd begun describing to him some of the content of the Tibetan Book of the Dead, and how unwillingness to recognise as our own the brilliant white light of pure being leads us straight into the arms of the Lord of all Terrors and rebirth in one of the realms of conditioned existence, all of which are pervaded by suffering, the worst being the hell realm which seemed to outdo even the worst of the medieval Christian visions of hell. As we'd lain in the dark while I explained that these things weren't just presented as mandatory beliefs but as actual psychic principles latent or manifest in one's own mind, Joe had jumped up shouting, "For fuck's sake man! Turn the frigg'n light on!" At which point we'd both burst out laughing at ourselves, our hair almost standing on end. Now I joined in with the laughing once again as I remembered it, and wondered how he was.

One of the footballers took a long shot that sent the ball spinning through one of the makeshift goals towards me. I reached forward and gathered it up, then kicked it back to them.
"Cheers mate," one of them shouted.
I waived and they resumed their game.

In my mood of self-recrimination, which by now was becoming a constant, I had broadened a fledgling interest in psychology that had been prompted by my fascination with a horrific recurring nightmare I had had since childhood.

Now I had begun to embrace psychotherapy, and had become aware of America's west coast scene, which included Fritz Perls' Gestalt therapy, and the various projects centred on the Californian Esalen Institute. I bought two of Perl's books – 'Gestalt Therapy' and 'Gestalt Therapy Verbatim'. The first was divided into two halves, one being theoretical and the other consisting in a sequence of practical self-help exercises. The second book contained dialogues between Perls and his clients. I read them both avidly and tried to put them into practice. I wanted to overcome my imperfections and become a better person, although what 'a better person' might be was a prejudice that I had unwittingly derived from other people's opinions, such as that one should be tolerant of other people's differences, that we should not be possessive in love but let our loved ones be free, that we should be self-reliant and not indulge jealousy and dependence on others, and so on. I wanted to be like that, and at school had dreamed of living in a commune with my male and female friends – one big hippy family. I wanted to become strong so that I could take my place amongst my peers and walk tall. So I had been knuckling down to the job and trying out the Gestalt therapists' suggestions. Perls had devised an approach partly derived from Freud's psychoanalytical insights into repression of the passionate instinctual self, the id, by one's conscious psychologically acceptable self, the ego, and particularly by that structure within the ego that Freud called the super-ego, one's conscience, derived mostly, according to Freud, from the moral authority of one's parents, especially from one's father who was usually the boss of the family. Given that we were all of these – id, ego and super-ego – and that therefore different aspects of ourselves were in conflict with each other, Perls came up with an exercise which might allow these aspects to enter into dialogue with each other in the hope of achieving reconciliation. The unconscious id, insofar as it revealed itself to the ego through its influences upon it, could find its voice in the ego alongside the super-ego, so that the two could relate to each other. Perls gave the participants names – Topdog and Underdog – and encouraged you to first be one and then the other, each voicing to the other its frustrations and grievances. I tried this, usually in writing as this seemed the best way to externalise it without the dialogue degenerating into a confused forgetful ramble. But sometimes I just spoke it out loud, talking to myself – a habit I still have today that has often drawn strange looks from people when I have apparently been chattering to myself in the car! You don't have to worry about that as much now that mobile phones and Bluetooth earpieces have become ubiquitous. You can imagine the conversation:

"Eigh, look at that nutter."
"Where? Oh don't be horrible John. He's just on the phone."

Again the football rushed towards me, curving to one side before lodging itself under the bench. One of the boys came running up, looking at me a little uncertainly.
"Was it a goal?" I asked.
"Yeah," he grinned.
I reached under the bench, rolled the ball out and punched it to him.
"Thanks," he said as he ran off, dribbling it back to his friends.

So the way it would go would be that first something would be bothering you about yourself – why else would you be doing this? It wouldn't be a physical thing which you could go to the doctor or the VD clinic about, something I'd had to do not long after being with Gwen as I'd got an infection of some kind. NSU they called it – non-specific urethritis – which seemed more or less to mean that you'd got what you already knew you'd got – an infection of some kind – but not one of the main venereal diseases. I presume the term 'venereal disease' has come to be regarded by today's guardians of public sensitivity as somehow too negative, linking in one term, as it does, disease and sexual love. Heaven forbid that health professionals might perpetuate any idea of sex being dirty! Now we must speak of STDs – sexually transmitted diseases – promoted in the hope that changing the name would change our attitudes to the problem. It has. Nobody feels any shame about venereal disease anymore, but neither do we feel ashamed of the sexual promiscuity that facilitates its transmission. Now we depend upon condoms and antibiotics in place of the disciplined moral propriety that used to safeguard us previously, neglect of which often exacted a corrective price in the form of venereal disease, just one among many of that neglect's consequences. I don't recollect anyone who associated venereal disease with sexual love as such. We associated it with sleeping around, a lesson which today's supposedly liberal establishment evidently finds politically unacceptable and seeks to suppress. Anyway, with NSU you ended up with the same treatment as VD proper – a course of antibiotics which usually did the trick. But there was no course of medicine that could cure the inner psychological conflict that was troubling me. Indeed there was no disease as such to be cured. The experience of inner conflict is essentially a state of indecision in which one is torn between two sets of possibilities and the desires to achieve them. As long as the indecision remains, the respective desires remain too, pulling against each other, disturbing the composure of one's whole being.

So you'd start somewhere – anywhere – just to get the thing going and give you something to work with:

Underdog – I've had enough of this. I'm sick to fucking death of it. I'm always behaving myself and not doing what I really want to do!

Then you'd take the other side:

Topdog – Well what is it that you really want to do?

Then you'd take it from there:

Underdog – I want to stop Gwen seeing Nicky.

Nicky was the friend she'd been to see, and who for all I know she'd gone and fucked.

TD – Why do you want to do that?
UD – Because I want her to want me, not him.
TD – Why? What's the problem?
UD – I don't want her to leave me for him.
TD – Isn't that for her to choose?
UD – But what about me?
TD – Shouldn't you just accept her choice?
UD – Yes but . . .
TD – But what? Do you believe in freedom or not?

UD – Yes but . . .
TD – Then bite your lip and toughen up!

Something like that anyway. But the reality was that I was deeply torn by the demands I was placing on myself in the name of freedom, tolerance, and non-violence. Perhaps because of all the bickering and unhappiness that had afflicted my Mum and Dad when I was growing up, when I first came across notions of communal living I was immediately taken with the idea as an alternative to the oppressive confinement of the nuclear family. But in my naivety I had never given any serious thought to what this might mean for the sexual fidelity that I had taken completely for granted between my parents and my other family members, and which provided me with so much security in my life when I most needed it. Now I was beginning to learn its value the hard way. Whether Gwen had actually had sex with Nicky or not, the presumption was that it was none of my business one way or the other. And that tormented me. And the more it tormented me, the more I blamed myself for failing to live by my own principles – which, as it happens, though I hadn't realised it at the time, were *not* actually my own principles.

Throughout this period and for long afterwards, I kept an increasingly fraught and chaotic journal, the contents of which give some idea of the torment I was going through:

October 30th, 1972 – I'm living in Exeter and enjoying myself.

December 7th – Have moved into a house on Western Road. Living with Gwen and Denny (and Dan Hicks and Jimi Hendrix and Tim Buckley . . .)

Dec 19th – Next year I don't want any shitty jobs, and I don't want to be signed-on as a general labourer at the Labour Exchange. And I don't want to get my hair cut. I want to love Gwen and I want to make things and be creative, because I think I'm good at it.

I was angry about the length of my hair because after having already worked there for a week without anyone saying anything about it, I'd just been sacked by the Social Security office for it being too long.

Jan 13th, 1973– I had my first nightmare for years last night – and it really was horrible! Don't know how seriously to take it yet.

Jan 18th – Where are the holes in my personality? Everywhere. You underestimate yourself. Sorry. Don't do that. What? Say "Sorry" like that. Like what? Like: "Sorry I should have known better," or "Sorry, but I had to give a modest impression." Christ!

Jan 24th – Fucking talk about sex and relationships! Talk, talk, mind-fucking talk! I fuck you! I don't want you to fuck anybody else when you're fucking me! How can you have 'free' sex without depersonalisation? I just don't see how it's possible.

Jan 25th – Back to the music. It's where I can cope. Gwen you're a fucking hypocrite and you're fucking me up. You say love is free but it's your bed we do it in, even when its mine! I love you – I don't give a shit about you! You're selfish. We're all selfish. Fuck you, FUCK YOU, FUCK YOU, FUCK YOU!

Jan 26th – Last night Nicky turned up, and that was about all I could take. A house for three, two dossers – one of whom Gwen "loves in a way", two more guests, too many cigarettes, too little sleep, me as jealous as fuck, and Gwen knowing it and resenting it, which made me even more jealous because now I felt she'd humiliate me by telling Nicky. I split to my room and waited – until after two in the morning. Denny came and kept me company for a while. My friend. My good friend. Then she came and we made love. I felt love for her different from before. Never felt it like that until then.

And so it had gone. Until by now exhaustion had sapped my bones and frayed my nerves. I couldn't bear to be with it all the time, and so only the week before, I'd gone to Bristol with Denny to get away from it and score some dope. When we'd got there Denny's dealer friend had nothing but a plant growing in a window box. Not wanting to disappoint, he'd cut it down and chopped it up, then put it in a pillow case.
"Do you want to wait here a while?" he had asked.
"Sure," Denny had replied.
Then he'd taken the pillow case to the launderette and tumble-dried it for a few cycles. When he'd come back he'd rolled a joint with it for us to sample. And darn it if it hadn't been probably the strongest grass we'd ever smoked! I'd been so stoned I hadn't even known what city I was in, and when we'd gone back to the coach station and were waiting to leave, I'd kept suggesting to Denny that we wait upstairs. But there was no upstairs! How the hell we got back to Exeter I really don't know. But we did. And thankfully when we did Nicky had gone and Gwen was on her own and glad to see us. "Thank God," I'd thought, breathing a sigh of relief.

But the grass really was strong, and so here I was, after a week of smoking it, sitting on a park bench trying to clear my head.

Despite the strain I'd been feeling in my relationship with Gwen, when she wasn't attending to old friendships or old flames, we continued to enjoy our adventitious coupling and spent many a merry evening with Denny and our friends. Eventually, when Phillip split up with Yvonne, he moved in with us, and eventually began to bring another girl – Susie – back to the house. She was a sweet educated Exeter girl – feminine, buxom and intelligent – very patient and caring of Phillip in his self-induced alcoholic stupidity. I liked her and found her sexy and was secretly envious of Phillip. I looked to Gwen, however, who took me to Manchester to meet a close girlfriend of hers, which reassured me greatly. And we planned to go travelling together during the coming spring, something I was able to look forward to which gave a sense of us having something of a future together. Meanwhile I got a job just down the road on Okehampton Street behind the Royal Oak, carrying out works to the river bank by the bridge. I joined a gang run by an attractive fore-woman not afraid to get her hands roughed up by the sand and cement of the concrete we mixed, and the cruel flinty splinters from the broken river pebbles we inset in the slop in the metal matrixes we'd put together to mould rows and rows of uniform geometric blocks. The blocks were designed to fit neatly together to create a hard-wearing attractive surface that while looking nice would not be easy to walk on, something some planner had deemed an improvement at this location.

As the weeks passed, along with the boozy nights, the music and the dope, another girl came to live at the house – Margot – who I later suspected of depriving me of my last week's pay before Gwen and I left for Tunisia. It was her or the postman – I never knew which. I didn't suspect her of dishonesty, but there was a vague unreliable vacantness about her that one couldn't trust. There wasn't anything I could do about it, however, and I still had enough money to be able to embark on our adventure.

Before the time came for us to set off, Gwen came down with German measles, and spent a week off work nursing her illness. After she'd recuperated she went to see Nicky once again – the perennial 'second string' it seemed, as he'd evidently been a presence in the background of her previous relationship.

March 3rd – Becoming very possessive. I must snap out of it.

April 8th – Just got back from Manchester. Seeing Beefheart wasn't as good as in Bristol. Poor hall acoustics. Got a letter from Marina, Pat and John. I've been made redundant. Shame. I'll miss Pat – crazy Irishman – with all his corny jokes and stories. And Marina, laughing while hating the work as much as the rest of us.

April 12th – Baked four loaves of wholemeal bread today. Tassajara Bread Book. Tastes fucking good. Will save a loaf for when Gwen gets back.

April 13th – Listening to Faust again. I miss Gwen. Hope I get a letter tomorrow.

April 15th – Sunday. Hugh wrote to tell me that Bridget St John and Michael Chapman are playing at Greenhead this coming Thursday. Last trip back home before we leave. Sunday slipped into Monday. Can't sleep because Gwen screwed Nicky and I'm not used to it. It's lovely outside. Sitting by the hissing gas fire at half past six. Dawn chorus subsiding. Gwen's sleeping. Lovely Gwen. How could I ever stop her from loving? I want to touch her and kiss her, but she'd wake up and get annoyed at my lack of self-control. I wonder how he screwed her?

I continued my journal entry by attending to the sensuality of the morning's progress as a way of distracting myself from my obsessive fears and anxieties, and the anger that accompanied them. I used my writing in this way to cut through my anguished thoughts and focus myself on those aspects of life that I felt I'd come here to enjoy. But I was using my idealism as a form of escapism, which, though understandable, was less than honest. The time hadn't come yet for me to realise this, however, and I struggled on, covering over the cracks with soothing reassurances of the fundamental goodness of life.

I made my Easter trip to Northumberland and said goodbye to my family, then came back to Exeter and Gwen in time to depart as we'd planned. We stayed in South East London for a couple of days with Hugh who was studying there, and met Eric who I'd meet again some years later, another friendship that has lasted until the present. Then we moved on to Gwen's parents' home in Kent for a night before travelling to the ferry for Ostend the following day.

8

April 29th – Duty-free Alfred Dunhill. Forty, no eighty. Yes, eighty. Milano stinks. It's shabby, and the young dudes at the station are a pain. It's Sunday evening. We set off on Thursday afternoon on the three-thirty ferry. Hitched from Ostend to Frankfurt and got there by the next morning. The first lift was from a Belgian who ran market stalls and owned a boutique. He gave us a good start but was a lousy driver. Then we got a lift off a Welshman to somewhere near the German border. Walk, walk, walk. Then a lorry to Köln, and another to Frankfurt through kilometres of forest. In my mind the Youngbloods:

You look to me
Like misty roses.
Too soft to touch,
But too lovely
To leave alone.

You look to me
Like love forever.
Too good to last,
But too lovely
Not to try.

Pretty picturesque German houses. Stop. Start. Stop. Start. Very tired. Hopped into a small Citroën to a service station, then a very fast lift in a ? to . . . another service station. Stuck for hours. Kicking leaves.

Nodding off against the trees. But then a lift to Freiberg and a household of hairy German students who were very friendly and put us up for the night. Car broke down the following morning while trams passed us by. Set off for Switzerland. Lift straight away to Basel, then Lucerne, then stuck in a little village below a pass that crossed over the Alps. Road closed. Ice thick on the road surface. Doubled back down country past Zürich and on to the San Bernardino tunnel, then down to Lugano on the lake. Northern Italy. Smelly and brash.

April 30th – Train to Rome – a rest from the hitch-hiking. Rome is better than Milan. A lot better. But I'm sure the pizza places keep ripping me off. Too many cars! Can't even cross the street safely on a zebra-crossing. Got beds in a cheap hotel. Free shower. Americans talking about Watergate.

May 5th – We went to Sicily, which was even shittier than Italy. Concrete roads. Mile after mile after mile. Cholera outbreak in Tunisia, so we hitched back up Italy to cut across to Brindisi – the heel of the Italian boot – and get a ferry to Greece. Corfu. It's clean and there aren't millions of cars. Lost my watch on the ferry, my Dad's present before I left. Not good.

Despite my scathing remarks about Italy and Sicily, the beauty of the landscape had still shone through the chaotic activities of the people, even though I had been shocked by their careless treatment and apparent lack of regard for it. Milan had been comparable to my memory of Leeds in its unnatural industrial mayhem. Everything had been oriented around the industrial economy, and was what I had been wanting and expecting to get away from. And even as we had headed south and the landscape had become more rural, it had still shocked me to see village dumps spilling debris and detritus down into what otherwise would have been quite beautiful little valleys with streams like those in Northumberland, filled with trout and home to so many other wild creatures. Yet despite all of this the sheer power of the landscape had come to the fore: the smell of oranges on Sicily and the trail of smoke rising from Etna; the massiveness of the mountains and the vast spaciousness of their morning skies; the kindness of the people and their pride in what was theirs, especially when they overlooked the embarrassing arrogance of our youth and treated us to their local delicacies – their breads and cheeses, coffees and wines.

On the road to Brindisi we passed a decapitated Alsatian dog – its torso in one place and its head in another. I remember the contrast between its black-brown coat and the livid pink of its torn blood-drained flesh, and the children standing nonchalantly nearby, looking into the car with smiling faces as we passed them.

Italy had been full of its own Mediterranean character, but I had only seen it from busy roads, weary for much of the time if not exhausted. And so nothing on our travels there prepared me for our approach to Corfu from the sea. Corfu back then, though beloved by many, was not the annual destination of the million or more holiday-makers that it is today. There was still more of Lawrence Durrell's 'Prospero's Cell' to it than Spanish beach resorts with their all too familiar high-rise hotels and crowded swimming pools. We caught the ferry in the evening when the air in Brindisi was still and tired after what in England would have been felt to be a scorching hot afternoon. Amid the preparations for its departure, the smell of diesel and exhaust fumes wafted up from service vehicles resupplying the ship, on air tinged with the fragrance of overripe gourds and decaying vegetables. We searched for a spot among the seated tables in one of the communal cabin areas where we might feel comfortable and agreeably situated, then we unburdened ourselves of our baggage and slumped down into our seats, glad of the change to something more solid than the tyres and bouncing suspension springs of the lorries and cars we'd been travelling in. Presently we felt a shudder pass through the vessel, then another, and then heard the idling hum of the engines crank up a pitch. The ferry began slowly to glide backwards and out into a channel where her path arced until we were adjacent to the quayside. Another small shudder signalled a reversal of the spin of her propellers, which brought her rearward drift to a halt and began her forward procession out of the harbour and into the night and the calm open sea.

We talked of the things we had seen that day, as the lights of Brindisi receded into the distance and the engine revolutions picked up speed. As we talked, we tore off pieces of bread from a loaf we'd bought from a mountain road café, and ate them with bits of broken cheese. We were tired, and tried to make ourselves comfortable enough to sleep during the hours to follow. We weren't due to arrive until the following morning, a long wait if we remained awake all that time. When our fellow passengers had begun to settle after the bustle of boarding, we took turns to visit the toilet to wash off the day's grime and sweat. I looked at myself in the mirror, saw the shadows under my eyes, and thought only of my pressing need to close them. When I got back, Gwen was already reclining with her eyes closed.
"Me too," I whimpered.
She smiled without replying.

In the springtime the ferries weren't crowded, and there was room to stretch out. My sleep was a series of sinkings into the deeps of oblivion, interspersed with moments of vague awareness of the ship's engines pounding away at her heart. Each resuscitation from slumber would fail to satisfy and I would be pulled back into the soporific comfort of unconsciousness, haunted by hints of experience and emotion. Eventually, while immersed in an eternity of timelessness, a chill came over me, and my eyes opened to see that the night had passed and been replaced with the subdued daylight of dawn. The sun had only just risen, and few people were awake yet. I shivered and sat up, and pulled a jumper and a crumpled white cotton jacket from out of my rucksack. Donning them, I stood up and walked out onto the gangway where I leaned against the side to look at the rippled sea and the blueing sky. The air was fresh and slightly scented – not with a sea smell, but with the smell of aromatic plant oils typical of Mediterranean lands. I looked to the front of the ship in the direction she was furrowing, but could see nothing but the horizon where sea and sky merged in a blurry haze. Inside the cabin, others were beginning to rouse and stretch. Most remained prostrate, but one man stood up and came outside.

"Kalimera," he said politely as he walked past me.

I smiled and nodded in return. He climbed a flight of stairs further down the deck, and disappeared onto the deck above. I walked back into the cabin, returned to my seat and picked up a book that Gwen had been reading. But reading it lulled me to sleep again and my head soon lolled against the cushioned seat-back. As I snoozed I felt Gwen's body move, and looked up to see her resting on one elbow. She greeted me with a murmur and a grin.

"Morning," she said drowsily. And after a pause inquired, "Did you sleep?"
I nodded. "Yeah. I couldn't keep my eyes open."
"What time is it?" she asked.
I looked down at my watch, but realised I wasn't wearing it. "Oh." I frowned, and realised with dismay that I must have left it by the wash basin the previous evening. I went to look for it but knew even before I did that it would be a waste of time. I came back looking disappointed and cross at myself.
"Not there?" Gwen asked in a tone of commiseration.
"No," I sighed, knowing it would disappoint my father more than me.
"Oh well," Gwen observed. "Nothing you can do about it now."
She was right. I didn't dwell on it, but instead allowed myself to be distracted by the quickening freshness of the air quickly warming as the sun climbed higher and shone more brightly. I looked around the seating area and noticed a clock on the wall.
"There you are," I said. "Seven thirty."
"Ah." She rubbed her eyes and took a bottle of water out from her bag to swig from it. "Want some?" she asked, offering me the bottle.
I reached across and took it, gulping down a few glugs.
"I wonder if there's anything to see yet, apart from sea?" she asked inquisitively.
"Not yet," I replied. "I looked."
She sat up and wrapped some toiletries in a towel.
"I'm off to the loo then. See you later." She smiled and stood up, stretching her neck and shoulders as she walked away.

Even inside the cabin I could sense the change. The ship now felt less like a Dover ferry and more like a Lakeland steamer, and even as it warmed, the air kept the same crisp clarity that it had always had in Northumberland when we'd stayed there with my Grandma in the school holidays. I could already feel the thrill of that joyful happiness that has always been my immediate response to Nature's beauty. It is not a beauty set apart from man that necessarily cannot include him, but one which he is properly a part of if only he will allow himself to live in harmony with it. It is that harmony itself, I think, which above all other kinds of happiness, is so profoundly pleasurable. Yet some people – many – have never known it, and having never known it, have never been nurtured by it, so that even in the midst of Nature they remain immune to her beauty and unmoved by it. I looked out through one of the cabin windows feeling the preciousness of the moment, and fearfully protective of what I so treasured. I wanted to drink it all in before it was too late, which I was sure it one day would be.

Gwen returned, now more awake and present. She put her things back in her pack and looked up. "I want to see," she said, peering through a window.
"OK," I volunteered. "I'll watch the stuff."
"Thank you," she piped. "Won't be long."
I watched her head pass by a window as she moved closer to the ship's bow, and could still see her in the one next to it as she lifted her hand to shield her eyes from the sunlight and looked around to see what could be seen. More people were lining the deck now and were tending to look in one direction more than any other. Gwen turned around and came back into the cabin.
"Come on," she beckoned. "Let's take these outside."

We lifted our packs onto our shoulders and carried them out to some benches fixed to the fore of the cabin where we put them down. In the distance ahead, a faint grey mass was becoming visible above the sea's surface, extending along it as far as we could see. As the ship progressed towards it and its magnitude disclosed itself, detail began to emerge, at first just the outline of land against the deep blue sky, but then differences in colour and texture which told something of the contours of what we were looking at. We were looking at mountains that dropped down close to a coastline and stretched out of view on both sides. But to the right, the mass was broken and the sea began to wrap around the break, revealing a separate mass which stood apart from the main one, surrounded by the watery expanse that so faithfully reflected the blueness up above. The ship steered a course towards the gap between the mainland and the land off its shores, all the while diminishing in stature as the two masses increased in theirs. We could see that the island, which was what this massif appeared to be, humped up highest at its northernmost tip, which the ship's wake would trace a path around before heading south off its eastern coast. Though we were filled with the anticipation of our imminent arrival, it would be another hour or more before we docked in Corfu town, and still the coast would continue on further than we could see. I would later learn that Corfu has roughly the shape of an east-facing sea horse, its head spanning around eighteen miles and its whole body-length just over thirty five. And as we could see as the ship's course took us closer, between the spires of cypress and the broad spreads of Holm oak, the island was overwhelmingly wooded with olive trees – many ancient and gnarled – which reached far up its rilled backbone, and the domed mount known as Pantokrator – after the Almighty – on the sea-horse's nose.

As the ship circled around not too far offshore, we were close enough to clearly see human settlement. It was not continuous but sporadic. In steeper locations the wooded covering came right down to the sea. In others, where the fluid surface of the barely tidal waters lapped against narrow beaches in small coves and along the edges of lesser gradients where the hills and peaks stood further back, rows or clusters of white-walled houses of different sizes and pattern, with tiled roofs the colour of terracotta, lined the coast here and there, those at the water's edge often having their own jetties suspended a few feet above the wavelets, with rowing boats or caiques bobbing alongside them, all painted with whites, reds and turquoisey blues. Dotted around among the trees higher up the slopes, patches of reflected light from the white walls of village houses would more closely match the sun's intensity than the grey-green foliage of the surrounding groves of olives or the even darker cypresses, which conveyed a sense of human life's elevated luminosity, refracted through those who had not just built these dwellings but had poured out the light of love upon them with their brushes and paints and their green-fingered coaxings of flowering pot plants that decorated verandas and staircases, or of climbers that scrambled over trellises and pergolas, their blossoms dripping down over patios like brilliant stringed jewels. For a moment I laughed at the almost clichéd perfection of it. Years later a Buddhist teacher who I followed for a long while, would similarly laugh as he explained of his own teachers' ways, "You always know what they're going to do – but it still always works!"

Eventually the landscape began to level out as we passed the sea-horse's throat and chest, and at last, instead of more picturesque villages, Corfu town came into view. As any guide to the place will tell you, Corfu is not just a Greek island, though it certainly is that. But also, at various times in its history, when not overrun by Muslim pirates from various parts of the North African coast, the island has been settled, governed, or otherwise influenced by Ilyrians, Corinthians, Peloponnesians, Athenians, Spartans, Romans, Byzantines, Vandals, Normans, Venetians, Bonapartist French, Tsarist Russians, Ottoman Turks, and Imperial Britains. And probably all of these influences could be seen in our first impressions of Corfu town, though only some would we have recognised. The harbour seemed to merge with old military ramparts built of stone, which dated back to the beginnings of the modern period when sixteenth century Corfu had been repeatedly attacked by the Turks who had dominated the rest of Greece. On a promontory to our left, and on raised ground to the right, were two ruined castles which overlooked the town. Its foot sat compactly between them behind a large elongated plaza whose sun-scorched well-trodden surface was crossed and bordered by roads lined with small bushy trees, which from various directions connected the town to the harbour front. One's first intimation of the character of the place was an assortment of awnings at the back of the plaza, which gave shade to tables and chairs at which both visitors and locals sat perusing the harbour's comings and goings. Stretching back from the road at the rear edge of the plaza and rising gently with the lie of the land, was an irregular matrix of narrow streets with tall terraces three or four storeys high, which had the same terracotta roofs as the village houses we'd seen.

The bow of the ferry soon gently approached the harbour wall alongside a jetty, its engines momentarily exerting themselves to halt the vessel's momentum so that it could be securely moored before lowering its ramp to let vehicles drive off at the front. Foot-passengers disembarked onto the jetty at the side, and after showing our passports to a uniformed official, and with nothing to declare and no great interest shown in us, we were soon walking on hot flagstones towards the plaza, seeing sights and smelling scents that I had never seen or smelt before.
"Let's have a wander," Gwen said brightly.
"Yeah!" I enthused.
We'd been cooped up on the ferry for hours and now revelled in our unrestraint. To us, the place appeared richly exotic, abounding in the charm of ages that in passing had left their indelible stamp, and now, like the weathered brickwork of an old house covered over with ivy or parthenocissus, gave domicile to the flora and fauna of new life so that everything conveyed the sense of having found its right and proper place, and of having assimilated the old to the new and vice versa – strange sentiments to feel, perhaps, in view of Greece's troubled and fractious modern history, and the fact to which at the time I was quite oblivious, that at that very moment the country had, for six years, already been governed by a military junta clandestinely promoted, it seems, by the American government whose CIA had recruited Papadopoulos, one of its generals, and intent upon suppressing ruthlessly wherever it seemed necessary, every political organisation that might conceivably be favourable to Soviet

communism. The Cold War at that time was a fact of life so engraved in everyone's minds that no one for a moment imagined that within two decades the Soviet Union would collapse, creating a very different world to the one responsible for all our hopes and fears back then.

But what were mine and Gwen's hopes and fears as we meandered through Corfu town's little alleys and streets, savouring their vibrancy and their fresh, sometimes pungent, aromas? To be entertained and invigorated by the island's charms? – by its old-world quaintness which we romanticised for what we felt was its as yet unbroken continuity with the Natural? Yes, yes. But in seeking these treasures in the Corfiots' land and way of life, how could we not impose both the sense and the nonsense of our own deficiencies onto them? We couldn't, and so we did. Unashamedly so. We naïvely hoped for 'love' and 'peace', and just as naïvely feared there would *be* none unless we made our youthful dreams come true. Yet Corfu's now crumbling castles and sea-facing ramparts, her narrow streets with their tall tenement buildings, many unpassable to vehicles other than motorbikes, scooters and mopeds, her harbour-front plaza whose dignified air reminded one more of one's besuited beloved old grandfather than of the fearsome authority of government whose officers would on occasion, perhaps, assemble and parade here, would once also have all been new and innovative, departing from what had been there before, and maybe at that time the subject of others' laments over the passing of the past with its old-world enchantments, and the inherent violence of the new. How could we not, without realising it, be the very worst kind of romantics – tyrannical in our nostalgic conservatism while at the same time ourselves being ambassadors of that innately revolutionary newness which would eventually transform Corfu to accommodate the heaving mass of tourists and holiday-makers that now annually descends upon her with much-needed money, but at the cost of having lost much of that original character and easily discovered solitude that had made her so appealing when first embraced by urban-industrial émigrés from the northwest? We were that, but we were blissfully unaware of it and blinkered by our youthful idealism, which typically envisaged as its ideal a world which does not suffer the imperfection of contradictions and conflicts. And there's the rub: the harmony of one's ideal world tends subtly or blatantly to include oneself, whereas the real world – the acceptance of which is a prerequisite of human maturity – need not. It can get on very well without us and indeed sooner or later requires our demise to do so, if only to make way for others. Whether our vacation occurs sooner or later is something we care very much to affect. We strive to include ourselves, through enmity if not through friendship. And whichever way it is, either you or the others are going to have to endure sacrifice. Harmony there may be, but it will always require individual sacrifice. It's only a matter of when and how. Oh, how I have raged and struggled against this simple truth, determined to make my world my very own heaven on earth and at the same time everyone else's, which, despite the glimmerings of sobriety that were beginning to impose the costs of sanity upon my wakening adulthood, is what I still was doing as I tramped those streets and delighted in its confectionaries and baked stuffs and hardware stalls and laundries.

May 6th – Still in Corfu town. Saw a nice hat in a shop near the seafront, but it was 60 drachmas and I felt I couldn't afford it. When I began to walk away, the shopkeeper knocked it down to 40 but I still didn't want it. Felt I ought to save my money for more important things like oranges and bread. Arms are beginning to tan. Prick beginning to cool off. White trousers beginning to show dirty smudges. If I were to turn around I'd be facing a column in the Doric style – one of twenty. Hippy bells jingling behind me somewhere. Dog's feet pitter-pattering on the paving stones. I bought a hand-line today. Thought I'd try to catch some fish with it as I'd watched a local youth catching plenty with one in the shallows along from the harbour yesterday. Not as easy as he made it look! Hook fouled on sea-weed. Can't find the shrimps. Don't like using them as bait anyway. Last night we had a smoke off some Americans who'd got it from some Germans who got it off a guy who brought it from Afghanistan. Nice of them to share it with us.

May 8th – Left Corfu town now. Been walking through the olive groves. Ants! All over the place. Tiny ants, English-large ants, and fucking big ants the size of house-flies! Two ants balancing on two straws poking out of a Cinzano bottle. There's no Cinzano in it – just water. Most of the ants are black, but a little red one has just crawled across the page, and I think one has bitten me below the balls! We had a vegetable stew last night, and the night before. Will have another tonight I expect. The sun is very hot, and I think I may be burning. The sea wasn't too hot though. In fact it was cold, but I think it will be warm now. "Twenty Proto, please." "Seex drachma." "Thank you." "Efharisto." The shiny pot was 24 drachma, but it isn't silver shiny anymore. It's black shiny – wood-fire shiny, reflecting a yellow sea with two red blotches. Two stone-walled hovels cemented with thick mud. Disused by the looks of it unless they're being used as barns. Not at the moment though. Disturbances in the night. Slept out in the open on a leafy patch below an olive tree. Woke up with a start! Was it a snake on my chest? Donkey snuffling among our rucksacks. Fucking donkey! Guffaws. Relief. "No time to lose." Three o' clock shuffle. Sleep it off. Sun shining. Maybe I am going to burn. Such a lazy writer. First time I've lifted a pen for days and look what's coming out. Shit! Absolute shit! Can't see any sense in it. Wasting the biro in fact. Black pot shiny lid. This is the way I write. Black pot shiny lid.

I was dozing off, different strands of thought becoming intertwined until they were no more than trains of fleeting impressions and snatches of conversation. The previous night we'd gone to sleep under a canopy of olive branches, watching fireflies flit among the leathery leaves and twigs. I'd not gotten enough sleep, having woken up in a panic when the weight of the snake that had entered my dream had suddenly seemed terribly real. When I'd opened my eyes it had been early morning, and the weight on my chest had been a donkey's nose, its big eyes looking down at my little ones looking back up! I'd laughed and then dozed some more, but the morning sun had soon made lingering repose cocooned in our sleeping bags stifling and uncomfortable, and the prospect of rising became far preferable. We'd rubbed our eyes and sat around half asleep for a while, our conversation moving slowly and punctuated by long gaps. The olive trees had not been too densely planted here, and around us had spread a carpet of spring flowers. The donkey had wandered off, and eventually so had we.

It seems an overstatement to describe our journeyings as 'hiking', as on our bare feet both of us were wearing nothing more than sandals. But walk we did, with our packs on our backs, going nowhere in particular except into an intimacy that couldn't have been experienced in any other way. We met with the moods of the countryside as the day progressed, and observed routines of peasant life that many Corfiots still lived. When we saw people, which in little villages and hamlets wasn't often, except for the widows the women usually wore loose black skirts and white blouses, and cotton headscarves to keep the sun off. They acknowledged us inquisitively with generous smiles when encountering us while going about their activities. The men looked much like my Mum's father, with flannel pants and old, often collarless, suit-shirts. Their well-worn waistcoats were trained to their wearers' bodies, and their flat caps seasoned over the years spent upon their owners' heads by sunlight, sweat, dust, leaf-litter, fish-slime, brine, olive sap. One had the sense that just handling and smelling a man's cap could give you intimate knowledge of who he was, the life he'd lived, and where he had lived it, while the freshness of the women' clothes or occasional lack of it, was as good as an invitation into their homes, and told you of the conditions of their spirits. Pride and dignity were the qualities that stood out above all, obliging their bearers to honour their humanity in ways which befitted the circumstances. We were strangers – foreigners – walking through their lands, and they were hospitable and kind to us, which, rationally-speaking, they had no need to be. Yet they were. For although we encroached on what they had made theirs, we were still human like them, and they were proud of their efforts. The more we enjoyed what was theirs, the happier and prouder they felt, the only condition being our gratitude and respect for their generosity. Had we not shown this they would have thought we were ailing in some way. Then their fulfilment of their human duties would have taken on a different cast – still honoured, but carried out with sadness, perhaps, or even bitterness and resentment. I remember one occasion on another visit many years later, when that dignified Corfiot spirit rose up against one of my British kinsfolk – a young woman filled with the very different spirit of consumer rights, making a hue and cry in the early hours of the morning having arrived at our small hotel off a delayed airline flight when all the guests were sleeping. After a while the proprietor got up to attend to her, but first barked, "Be quiet Madam! You're in my country now! This is not London!" Later, at breakfast, no one congratulated him more as he went from table to table taking orders than his British guests! "Well done, well done!" we said discreetly. It was we who we were all trying to get away from, and the woman's cultivated self-righteous sense of grievance had painfully reminded us of ourselves.

As Gwen and I ambled along amidst that rustic jumble of stone walls, parched stony meadows, and the ever-present groves of black-barked olives, we began to tire, our initial light-stepped striding gradually settling into a laboured trudge. Approaching midday, as the road led past a gaggle of modest old village houses, a cheerful wifely woman noticed our weariness and took pity on us. She spoke no English but smiled and beckoned us to follow her into a simple almost empty room with rude stone walls not greatly more elaborate than those that had enclosed the occasional parcels of land we'd passed, which people had troubled themselves to demonstrate in that way their possession of. In the room's shade, there were a couple of wooden chairs which she gestured towards, inviting us to sit. We beamed and thanked her profusely. She nodded, and again using hand gestures, indicated her wish that we remain while she leave momentarily. After a while she returned carrying a lacquered wooden tray from which much of the lacquer had worn off or been bleached by the sun. On it she'd placed a jug and two tin cups.

"Hah," she uttered, pouring some of the jug's contents into the cups and offering them to us.

"Thank you!" we blurted. "Thank you very much!"

We drank what seemed to be a cordial of some kind, unsure as to its peculiar flavour.

"Heh?" she quizzed, expectantly.

"Mmmm!" We grinned and nodded our approval. "Very good! Very nice! Thank you."

"Ey," the lady murmured, cocking her head to one side, evidently satisfied that her attempt to refresh us had achieved its purpose. She nodded and lifted her palm towards us as she walked away holding the tray.

"How lovely!" Gwen exclaimed.

"Yes," I agreed.

"And this place!" Gwen continued, "It's so pretty!"

We could dimly make out the underneath of the roof tiles in the shadows above us, and sat for some time in the stillness, peering out through the open doorway where the sun was baking the exposed ground, searing the stones and rocks until they were barely touchable.

"God. Imagine living here!" Gwen said, rolling her eyes and shaking her head in wonder.

"Amazing!" I agreed.

We sat a little longer until we felt rested, then found the lady to thank her, bowing towards her and smiling. She in return spread her palms towards us, hands upraised, while returning our smiles and shaking her head.

And so we set off once again, soon to be shaded by the olives. We didn't talk much. We were too interested in what we were seeing and smelling. Now and then we attracted the other's attention to point something out, then pressed on to nowhere but the next thing of interest. Meanwhile the sun slowly crossed the sky, altering the mood of the land, and as the afternoon passed and evening approached, the movements of the air settled and the light

took on a flat quality. When the sun finally disappeared behind the island's spine, and only the distant Albanian mountains captured the remaining reddening glow of the day's last rays, we noticed coming towards us an elderly man of seventy years or so, his tanned face wrinkled and whiskery, his eyebrows bushy and black. His advance towards us was slow and unmethodical. Rather, he kept turning towards the trees and scouring the ground with his gaze, sometimes stepping off the road and stooping to pick things up. As he came closer we could see that under one of his arms he was carrying a bundle of twigs and small dead branches. When eventually he noticed us he saluted and grinned. His boots were worn out and shabby and the soles were coming away from the uppers at the toes. The fabric of the army tunic he was wearing was threadbare and frayed at the elbows. As he lowered his arm to his side while still puffing out his chest, he greeted us with a nod and said, "Kalispera," which means 'good evening'.
"Kalispera," we replied.
He looked up between the olive branches taking measure of the fading light, then picked up a last piece of firewood before turning and directing us to follow him.

It wasn't long before we came to an old stone hut with just a door and no windows. He waived us in behind him as he entered into the gloomy interior. By what little light entered through the open door, we could see that there was nothing inside except a blanket and a stool to sit on, and at one end a roughly made hearth blackened with ashes. Beside it stood a small conical pot of the kind Greeks used to make coffee in, and next to it a dented old canister filled with water. The man laid his bundle down and from inside his tunic took out a posy of freshly picked jasmine blossoms.

He chuckled as he shuffled around in the half light, while behind him we squatted silently on the uneven slab floor. Heaping the smaller twigs onto a nest of dried grass, he lit a fire with a beat-up old brass lighter, then put on some of the heavier branches. The air in the hut became smoky and choking and started to sting our eyes, but politeness prevented us from leaving. There was no chimney, and the only way the smoke was able to escape was through the many gaps between the roof tiles. As the flames rose and illuminated the walls with their flickering light, hanging above the hearth we saw a framed photograph of a man of evidently high status, wearing a decorated military uniform. His impassive face looked out from the portrait with an air of paternalistic gravity. The old soldier noticed us looking up at it and immediately stood up and saluted it, stamping his foot hard down on the ground. Then he sat down again, nodding towards us proudly, before reaching over to drop the blossoms into the water canister and placing it on the burning embers. He said nothing, but just gazed into the fire, waiting for the brew to begin steaming. When the surface began bubbling he poured some of the tea for himself into the conical pot and passed us the canister to share between us. The scent of the jasmine blended with that of the wood smoke as we waited for the tea to cool. I looked at our host and sighed, not out of pity, but out of the sense of having been humbled by a spirit far humbler and more generous than mine. He'd shared with us what was his, and what was his was no more than what God had given him – a few blossoms off a tree, a fire, some water, a shelter for the night. And to the patrician in the photograph he appeared to have given his whole life in exchange for very little. There were no words that could do justice to this ageing man's beauty – whatever his political views. And so it was fitting that we sat with him in silence, listening to the crackling of the twigs as the flames consumed them.

That evening we'd stayed on the hard stone slabs in homage to our host's kindness, and as best we could had surrendered there to our need for sleep. We'd woken early before him, and had pushed open the door to let in some light and some fresh air. We looked at him lying on his dusty blanket near the hearth, motionless except for the rising and falling of his chest.
"He's fast asleep still," said Gwen softly.
We decided to let him be, and carefully gathered our things and went outside where we splashed some water on our faces and rubbed the sleep out of our eyes. We took a few swigs from the bottle we had with us, then picked up our packs and moved on.

Our travels took us through more olive groves and more pockets of habitation as the hours progressed through their daily cycle, but gradually our path led us back down to the sea where we spent the afternoon on a long sandy beach, and picked through the driftwood and the sea shells, avoiding the occasional globule of tarry crude oil. Without a care for the routines of ordinary work-bound life, we let ourselves be taken over by the routines of Nature instead, the quiet power of whose endless repetitions immersed us in a sense of timeless continuity that tempered the distractions and excitements of our particular lives. There was a persistent breeze and the sea was choppy, tossing about more than usual the little fishing boats and the caiques taking holidaymakers on excursions to remote islets and beaches.

"Do you think you know what they're on about when they talk about the 'void'?" I asked Gwen. "The Buddhists – and Kerouac – I mean."

Gwen paused and looked out across the water.

"Sort of, I think."

She kept looking into the distance.

"Well?"

"Well – I think it's the stillness of things – the centre."

I pondered what she'd said.

"Yeah, maybe that's it. I'm still trying to understand it."

We still had in common the feeling that what we were experiencing right there and then was real and beautiful, and that the life we'd been prepared for by our years at school – the job, the family, the car, the years spent in bondage to the debt needed to pay for them – took one away from it. It seemed a miserable prospect, and one we wanted to avoid. And what it said about the society we'd been born into, and the wars it fought and tried to justify, was something we didn't want to have to hear. But right here, where work and play, practicality and beauty, appeared to effortlessly penetrate one another so that one didn't have to choose between them, this seemed to be it, the whole point of it all – the good life. If only we could live like this back home. We wanted to live a *real* life, and, as Joni Mitchell had put it, 'get back to the garden'. Our desire for beauty was beautiful in itself, and immensely sensual and pleasurable, to the point of intoxication. Sometimes the sensuality was so rich, and the accompanying pleasure so intense, that one could hardly bear it, and felt the need to draw back from it to sober up, or drink a few beers to ease the pace of it and wind ourselves down. Our stay in Corfu was lived as if on a holy summit at the end of an arduous pilgrimage, a Dionysian mystery cult without the tearing apart of the sacrificial goats. We followed our passions through the succession of discoveries we made of the island's landscape and people, and the ways the two accommodated each other, with one foot in past tradition and the other in present modernity. How long would it be, one wondered, before the advance of modernity became a deluge even here, and past tradition no more than a memory preserved in museums and hallowed church buildings, and in vestigial traces left in the local dialect? And *there* was the paradox of our posture: we prided ourselves on our being a revolutionary challenge to the alienation and exploitation of actual modernity, and yet we longed for the charm of an unspoilt past. But revolution is a break with the past, and if one breaks with the traditional ways of remembering it, then how can it be remembered? How else might its ways be resurrected in the present that we might enjoy those of its virtues we so admired? In the end it came down to revolutionary faith – faith that the revolution itself would find a way, by virtue of the new liberated consciousness that the revolution was bringing forth. With liberation, we believed, our humanity would emerge unfettered and pure, and that that purity would lead us to new ways of living in harmony with Nature. Thus we sought out everything that might be experienced as liberating or exhilarating, and lived as exorcists banishing whatever demons seemed to oppress or suffocate life's thirst for life. We sought out anything and everything that stimulated life, and were as happy dancing to Greek music under the tutelage of canny Corfiot bar-owners drumming up business, as we were combing beaches or climbing through the olives to the tops of the hills or mountains they were growing on. We went to the north to the slopes around Pantokrator, then went to the south with its flatlands and dune grasses and poisonous snakes basking in the sun. Then we returned north again to Sidari where we swam in the coves along with the regular kinds of holidaymaker who eventually would go back to their rooms to shower and freshen up, while we remained out in the open with the sand and salt on our skin, eyeing up places to encamp for the night. We had no schedule or deadlines to meet and could stay as long as we pleased. We'd even been offered jobs encouraging Greek dancing in one of the bars. Gwen fancied the idea and would have accepted, but in the end we still were who we were, and I didn't warm to it. I could see her wholeheartedly entering into the spirit of the thing, her attention to me overshadowed, while I tried to conceal a feeling of resentment. I was jealous of our circumstantial intimacy, and didn't want to end it by sharing her with groups of intoxicated fun-lovers. My reluctance to take the job didn't seem to bother her, however, and I was not honest enough, even with myself, to be able to admit to her the true reason for it. I just said I'd rather make our way back, which, without jobs, we'd have to as our money was running out.

The night before we left we spent in Corfu town, which had been overrun by the crew of an American aircraft carrier moored offshore. The sailors were friendly and had money to spend. We sat with a group of them in a taverna where we ate souvlaki and drank ouzo and retsina along with the beers. They were loud, talkative, and of every race. I sat next to a hip black New Yorker who was so hip, in fact, that I couldn't understand a word he spoke. I just had to follow the inflections of his drawl, and laugh when he did, and

hope he didn't notice that apart from our sympathetic exchange of emotions I hadn't the faintest idea what he was saying to me.
"Heh! Far out!" I'd say, with a belly laugh, or some other such utterance, whenever his mirth spilled over.
"Heh-heh!" he'd grunt.
I'd shake my head in a knowing manner. Wherever he was going with his vocal ejaculations, I was with him all the way!

The following morning we caught a ferry across to Igoumenitsa on the mainland, and began the business of securing a lift. As we tried to hitch out, a lorry coming in paused alongside us. The driver leaned out, and in broken English explained that eventually he would be heading up towards Yugoslavia, but not until six in the evening – he needed the rest. We jumped at his offer and climbed up into the cab, riding as far as the parking area where he said we could meet him later in the day. With some hours to kill we wandered about the town, but were disinterested due to the distraction of our imminent departure. As a counter we went into a cinema where we'd noticed 'The Battle of Britain' was playing. It was English, we reasoned, we'd understand it, so why not? It'd pass the time. We bought our tickets and sat virtually alone in the darkened theatre. Then the film began. The stirring patriotic music stirred our native patriotism, then Lawrence Olivier or whoever it was, said with the utmost gravity, something in Greek! The film had been dubbed and so the only dialogue we could understand was that spoken by the Germans, which had been sub-titled in the original film. The film was still terribly exciting, and not knowing what our compatriots were saying added a whole new dimension to it, and anyway, seeing Suzanna York take off her skirt and stand there in her stockings and heels while speaking in Greek to her lover, was a stimulating experience, even though it did remind me of sitting silently in the front room at home with my parents, feeling embarrassed at something sexual on TV. I wasn't sure how to react in this similar situation with Gwen there. Should I stay silent, as I had with my Mum and Dad? Or should I comment on it as if I was on top of it – which I wasn't? Before I decided, Gwen laughed.

"This is so silly," she whispered, as if I weren't the only other person there.

"Huh! Ridiculous!" I was relieved to agree, pretending unaffectedness.

By the time the film ended it was close to being time for our lift. We left the cinema and walked to the lorry park where we'd arranged to meet our man. He was there walking around the vehicle, inspecting it before setting off.

Our return journey was blessed with good luck. We caught single rides through Greece, Yugoslavia, Austria, Germany, and Belgium, making it back to Dover in four days. From the outset, the journey through northern Greece and Macedonia had immediately taken us up into mountains that ranged down all the way from Bosnia in Yugoslavia. The road traversed precipitous mountainsides with hair-raising overhangs on the frequent bends. Our progress was slow, and as night fell we allowed ourselves to sleep. When we eventually climbed down from the cab and thanked the driver for his kindness, we'd already crossed the border into Kosovo, and very quickly caught another lift that took us the length of the country. Here we'd courted another kind of danger when our driver, a tall stout young man, far stronger than I, had asked us using rude sign language if he could have sex with Gwen. We'd pretended we hadn't understood, and hoped he'd be put off by our apparently clueless innocence. He could easily have broken my back and had his way with her, but, whatever dark thoughts he may have had, I think he'd been basically just a frustrated but good-hearted young fellow trying his luck, and thankfully his innate goodness won the day. He'd made no more of it and continued to share his food with us. After him we pressed on in a fast saloon car through Austria, and down towards Germany along a deeply cut river valley gouged out of the rock by a seething river whose brown boiling waters raged against their containment while flowing ever-onward to their certain destination. Then Deutschland with its GI Joes and white stars. Then Belgium, Ostend, the heaving Channel, and England.

Back in our homeland we stayed with Gwen's parents for longer than I might have wished. It was an anti-climax that frustrated me, alleviated only by a visit to Hugh up in London. Her parents were kind to me, and her sister as tolerant as could reasonably be expected of a younger sister of her age. One evening before we left, Gwen made more noise than usual when we had sex, knowing full well that her parents in the next room could hear. I didn't like it, and felt I was being used for a purpose I didn't care to know about or understand. When at last we set off for Exeter, my relief was long overdue. Our rides skirted London's suburbs before we headed west towards Devon through Surrey, Hampshire, Wiltshire and Dorset. The going was difficult and the lifts hard to come by, and by the time we tramped up to the front door of our Exeter house we were exhausted and ready to flop.

9

It wasn't long after we got back before the trouble started. It was great to see Denny again, and we soon resumed our lives together and fell into our old ways with the dope and the drink, regularly doing both at the weekly art college bops. Spring was turning into summer, and my bread-baking was becoming more than just a household thing but turning into something of a cottage industry supplying loaves to neighbours and friends as well as meeting our own needs. I began selling to a wholefood shop that had set up on North Street, and eventually took advantage of their two big ovens, baking there in far larger amounts than I was able to in our domestic kitchen on Western Road. All the while, as this dimension of my life was unfolding, so too was another: the therapeutic practices that I had been exploring were beginning to have life-changing effects, and as they did I became more and more dissatisfied with the life I was living with Gwen and Denny and the others. It seemed odd at the time, but Gwen didn't resist much the direction our relationship was taking.

"I'm outgrowing you," I once said to her, which might have been taken as a rather offensive expression of arrogance. But Gwen had merely replied,
"I know."
I began to realise that she didn't know much at all about where my mind was moving *to*, only where it was departing *from*, which, for reasons quite obvious to me now, was where she wanted to stay. The psychology behind gestalt therapy had made tremendous sense to me, and effected my understanding of myself as emotionally undernourished and correspondingly malformed. I hadn't seen this as a purely personal problem, but as a general one which happened to have affected me. My present friends and acquaintances, however, seemed quite unperturbed by what felt to me to be a matter of great urgency. Instead, they carried on as usual in the same old vein, and I began to feel increasingly isolated within my own social circle. I seemed to be alone in wanting to radically change myself, the others appearing to me to be too self-satisfied and complacent. For them, the old routines seemed adequate for the fulfilment of their desires, whereas for me, they were not. But I was an idiot too for not realising that for them it was all about sex. I was presenting an opportunity by vacating the field, and they responded accordingly in keeping with the social situation and the mores of the time. There was nothing malicious in it. It was simply an inevitable consequence of the factors at work that we were committed to. I was creating an opening, the filling of which naturally became the most pressing issue for them. My isolation was my own doing, and was my first conscious encounter with the lonely exclusiveness of personal responsibility.

Fritz Perls' introduction to gestalt therapy, written with Ralph Hefferline and Paul Goodman, had been subtitled 'Excitement and Growth in the Human Personality', and had focused greatly on the ways in which the formation of our emotionally meaningful perceptions tends to be interrupted and arrested due to various influences brought to bear during our developments. As a consequence of these we become indisposed to letting our perceptions of things, and our feelings about them, come together properly to achieve their full stature. We interrupt them before we've completed them, so that our insights into ourselves and our world remain immature and over-dependent on others who we look to to compensate for our immaturity, as if they were surrogate parents. Having become familiar with the picture, the pieces had all fallen into place and were beginning to make sense of my experience of myself, but the final dawn of profound recognition came when I read Arthur Janov's 'The Primal Scream'.

As always, we'd been smoking dope routinely and allowing ourselves to be transported by music to imaginary vistas that confirmed our chosen identities and explicated the emotional possibilities implicit in them. Implicit in mine was a fatuous overconfidence in the freedom and efficaciousness of imagination itself, as if it were the only significant limit on what one could achieve in the world. It had been a sort of faith with me, an extension of childhood playfulness. What could be more satisfying than imagining a better life for oneself – better circumstances, more beautiful relationships with things – and then striving for these in one's real life? The formula would be perfect were it not for the fact that one's imagination tends to compensate for one's own deficiencies, and as a consequence is correspondingly unrealistic and unachievable. Because of this, following its lead can set one headlong on a course towards personal crisis and disaster. In an imperfect world, to grow up with parents is in part to grow up without them, and it's in the gaps – the absences of perfection – that we're on our own, making it up as we go along. Our free will alone ensures that neither our parents nor anyone else will be adequate to the task of providing us with all that we need, so that as we grow in body and mind, others' role becomes more that of providing friendship, and, if we are fortunate, providing guidance and help in facilitating our own adaptation to reality. In childhood and infancy, however, whether through the intrinsic imperfections of Nature, or those caused by unnatural wounds, we are liable to suffer from our parents' negligence or inability to satisfy our wishes, and when those wishes express deep-seated needs, what we suffer is more than just frustrated instinct as Freud thought of it, but rather, the terrible wounds of self-deformation and destruction, what Janov called 'primal pain'. He entitled his first book on the subject after possibly the most common way of expressing it – screaming – which reflects the agony of being deprived of one's true self. There is in Janov's theory, a presumption of conscious self-interest, in which one loves, desires and seeks with all one's heart, this personal reality.

I read Janov's book one mid-summer's day, and I knew as I read it that what it was saying was true. I'd virtually finished it by late evening, and by then was experiencing a fusillade of insights, each flashing in my brain like a shell-burst, dissolving the emotional and ideational stitches that had been holding my adopted comportment together. As each stitch gave way it loosened the next, so that the whole garment of habitual attitudes and emotions began to come apart. Except for Gwen, who was away at the time, everyone in the household had gone to bed. As I sat in the kitchen at the back of the house, I felt I was experiencing a psychological earthquake. I closed the book and pushed it away from me, looking at the painting on its cover – 'The Temptation of St Anthony'. I punched the air with my clenched fist and silently voiced a triumphant cry of defiance against my father.

"No, no, no!" I protested. "Never again! I'm me! Me! You fuck off!"

With that, an outpouring of relief combined with an avalanche of feelings of righteous indignation and anger, became unstoppable, and as it proceeded, my sensitivity to my points of contact with the world became acute. It was as if a switch had been flipped and had turned on my whole being, transforming it from semi-conscious somnambulist to wide awake aesthete. Suddenly, from within the kitchen, I could smell the scent of every blossom out in the gardens behind the terrace. I was no longer remembering my past as a collection of filed facts, referenced and ready to retrieve, but was actually remembering myself whole once again, restoring abandoned and forgotten parts of myself and reconnecting them to my consciousness. I was radiant with wonder, filled with the happiness and joy of a homecoming in which one reacquaints oneself with everything one once loved and treasured and unreservedly entrusted oneself to. This new world that I was discovering was just the old one that I had insulated myself from, the reality of which had now broken through that insulation and called me back to itself. And once the breach had been made, my primordial self had leapt through like a long-incarcerated convict grasping at freedom the moment the opportunity had arisen, or two lovers seeing each other for the first time after a long separation, unable to resist rushing towards each other to re-unite in passionate embrace. I felt that I was the world's lover, and that she was my consort. I opened the kitchen door and walked out to the untended garden where I twirled like a ballerina on the dry exposed soil, and looked up at the stars and the moonlit clouds with a huge open-mouthed grin. I'd been lost to myself and had now found myself again, and felt like a mother who'd found her lost child, or a child who'd found his lost mother. Gladness and joy! Gladness and joy!

It was two in the morning and drunk as I was with this unanticipated ecstasy, my eyelids were becoming heavy and I needed to sleep. I walked back into the house and closed the door, still smiling uncontrollably as I turned the key in the lock. Then I went up to my bedroom and lay down. I closed my eyes and everywhere there was the light of consciousness – absolutely everywhere! Was I awake or asleep? It hardly seemed to matter, for whichever it was I felt that nowhere was not lit up. As I pondered over it, the joyful aspect of my experience subsided in an instant, and was replaced by doubt. How could I sleep bathed in this brilliance? I was exhausted, but still it radiated like the sun, and was no more likely than it to stop doing so. It was inescapable. There were no clouds. There was no shade of ignorance anymore. How on earth was I going to sleep? I lay there for a while with that brilliance inside my head, then put on the room light, hoping that ordinary perceptions would provide a refuge from it. But all of them were lit up by it too. Yet this wasn't like the effects of LSD. This was an effect of me being me, but I felt I had never been so intensely myself before, except perhaps as a baby. Was this intensity the norm that I had been missing, and that I must get used to now that I had awoken it? Or was it an anomaly of some kind that I was experiencing? I wasn't sure, but it didn't feel alien. I recognised it. Somehow it was me, and belonged to me. And so I turned the room light off again, and lay there in the brilliant darkness before eventually slipping into brilliant sleep.

The moment I came to, I was immediately wide awake, and could hear pots and plates clanking in the kitchen downstairs. I looked around me and glanced out through the window. There the world was – incontrovertibly – solid, dependable, immediate and present. Straight away I felt a thrill of joy in response to the actual sun and the morning air, and wanted to get up and go out to play – as if I were seven years old all over again. Come to me, come to me, the world seemed to say! Yes, my heart replied! And I jumped out of bed to get dressed, before skipping downstairs and into the kitchen.
"Hi," said Den. "Sleep well?"
I hardly knew what to say.
"Yes, thank you," I replied.
"You look like shit," he observed.
"I feel great!" I said, contradicting him.
How could I explain to my dear friend what had happened? It was completely invisible to anyone else.
"I'm going through something amazing Den," I said to him.
He glanced across at me while peering under the grill at the slices of toast that were beginning to char and smoulder at the edges.

"Oh yeah?"
"Yeah. Amazing!" I shook my head.
"You've been smoking too much dope!" he chortled.
I joined in with a hearty but nervous laugh.
"No it's not that," I protested. "It's something else."
"Like what?" he asked, while scraping some of the burnt bits into the sink.
I searched my mind for a way to explain.
"Oh God, Den. I don't know. It's like I've been asleep and have woken up."
"You have been asleep and woken up!"
He guffawed again, and I joined in with him again.
"No, man. Seriously. It's like I've been asleep for years and I've suddenly woken up. Like Sleeping Beauty."
"You should be so lucky you ugly cunt!"
"Oh for fuck's sake Den!"
We both shook, and tossed our heads. Den buttered the toast and put a slice down in front of me.
"Here, man. Have a piece."
"Ta' Den."
His eyes smiled, the way they did when he wanted you to know that he was there with you, in spirit. He sat crunching his toast and looking in amusement at me without saying anything. I shook my head.
"Oh man, it's so hard to explain," I complained. I so desperately wanted to communicate to him what I was going through, but couldn't. Every attempt to explain it seemed so pathetically feeble that I kept cutting my sentences short and sighing in exasperation.
"Well, it's this therapy stuff," I began. "It's . . . it's . . . it's done something amazing!"
"Yeah . . . ?"

"Well, it's sort of blown my mind," I answered. "I don't mean, like blown a fuse. I mean, it's blown it wide open!"
"Are you OK?" Den asked, with a note of concern.
"Yeah, I think so," I replied. "I'm OK. But it really is amazing!"
I knew he didn't really know what I was talking about, but his concern was real, and I loved him for it. My friend. It was so good to have a friend.

I wasn't sure what to do with myself. It was like having a new body and not knowing quite how to use it yet. Everything I did felt new, and a little strange. And because everything now felt novel, no particular thing or prospect interested me more than any other. The world had become one continuous blast of interest-worthiness, each thing capturing my interest as powerfully as what had preceded it and as what was to follow. Was this good? Yes and no. There was a richness to it, but it was also somewhat debilitating in its unrelenting unfaltering tempo. Was this what God was like? Was it the Void? – the Tathagata? – Great Emptiness? – therapeutic gold? – a dope-induced car crash? Even if it was the latter, this did not necessarily invalidate its significance. Shamans the world over have used the psychotropic properties of plants and fungi to 'cleanse the doors of perception', as Huxley put it, to allow people to see and hear things as they really are – unashamedly naked acts of becoming, enacted by one not defined by those acts but only revealed by them, and existent before them. But if I was having my brain washed, it was, without doubt, a jet-wash – or so it felt, at least. And the only conceivable way that I might have adequately expressed that feeling, would have been to roar and bellow in some measure proportionate to the intensity of emotion associated with it – that, or just collapse prostrate in a state of surrender to it. An alternative, though, was to look at my emotions themselves, and try to understand why they were so intense. I suspected that they were adding a different kind of intensity to the purity of my perceptions, and that because of that I certainly wasn't 'naked and unashamed'. I was clothing God's work with my own opinions and attitudes. Yes, there had been a breakthrough, but the old citadel was still standing, and its armies were battling with those besieging it. Whose side was I on? Both sides. It's always that way. I *am* Legion, for we *are* many. Jesus said that a man cannot serve two masters, ultimately we have only one, and so if we serve another we are tormented by both. In the end, what's real is whatever is real, no matter how unreal we may wish to be. And when reality breaks into our world of fictions and postures, as it always must if only at the point of death, then whether its heralds appear as angels or demons depends on our willingness to surrender to its truth. If we can't, but continue to cling instead to our self-deceptions and our fabricated and therefore false sense of personal independence, then we feel as if another mind has entered our own, and that that mere presence within oneself conveys a rapacious sense of malevolence. Surrender or hell. It wasn't much of a choice rationally-speaking, but speaking rationally and behaving appropriately are two very different things, and the latter, once you've spent your life building up a body of habitual untruths and dishonesty, is hard to even want to do, and even harder to persevere in.

"I'm off to the shops. Fancy coming?" Den asked.

I felt my tummy muscles quiver a little, and my bowels contract.

"No, I think I'll stay here for now," I replied. "I think I need to crap."
He sniggered.
"OK, see you later."
He picked up his door keys and left.

I went upstairs to my room and looked out of the window at the sun-bathed gardens. I was trembling slightly, with goose bumps standing up on the backs of my arms. I lifted the sash an inch or two to let some air in, then opened the drawer of the bedside cabinet and took out the Gideon's New Testament given to me by my grammar school in Yorkshire when I'd first gone there: 'Then the devil left him and the angels ministered to him.' Persevere, I thought to myself. I wasn't sure if it made any sense at all to believe in the words I was reading, but I had associated them for so long with spiritual authority and solace that they still comforted me and gave me hope and courage, so much so that just to hold the book and hold its cover to my cheek and lips, and feel its India-paper pages crinkle crisply as I turned them, was a comfort – a still point of refuge in a world at war over my soul. I heard a cock crow not far away – one of the neighbours must have been keeping chickens. I read the beatitudes, and looked across at the cover of Janov's book. I got myself into this, I thought, and the only way out is through it. Persevere. This isn't a head trip. It's just energy. If it goes screwy it's me that's screwing it up, and I can unscrew it. I sighed and relaxed a bit, then went to the loo still holding the little volume of scripture.

In the afternoon we sat out in the back garden. The summer heat had made the weather muggy and thundery, with gunmetal grey clouds piling up into the heavens, and the sun's rays reaching down between them, gradually being absorbed by a thickening haze so that the world was blanketed by a diffuse white luminosity tinted with hints of fresh bruising. Wendy was there, and Phillip and Susie and Margot. Denny rolled a joint and passed it around. Wendy was laughing and smiling a lot, her face flushed with inebriation. Phillip, whose face was always red since he was almost always inebriated, had a can of beer in his hand, and looked like the happy drunk that he was. His tousled wheat-blond hair bounced about his head in wild springy coils.

"Alright Ced?" he inquired, lifting his can to toast me, and giggling inanely.

"Alright Phillip," I replied.

Susie gave a demure good-natured grin, her smooth young bosom creamy and inviting above the low neckline of her cotton top. It was usual on such occasions to amuse ourselves with playful observations and verbal acrobatics, and for the others there, this day was no different to any other. So the conversation twisted and turned and somersaulted and jumped through hoops, accompanied by applause, laughter and merriment. But for me it was a very different day to most others, since from the moment I had woken up I had been in a state of rapture, my sensitivities altered, both in focus and intensity. On this day, word play and mental gymnastics didn't interest me much, and indeed seemed quite irrelevant to me. I sat there like a small child in a young man's body, marvelling at the clarity of my sensuality and my perceptions.

As the afternoon progressed, the occasional rumble of thunder reached our ears from the far distance. Den, who must have begun to feel hungry, eventually disappeared into the kitchen and began busying himself there. After ten minutes or so, he came back and asked, "Spaghetti anybody?"

When we all enthusiastically replied, "Yes please!" he went to fetch some bowls and a bottle of wine. He put them down, went off again, and came back with some tumblers. "Vino?" he asked.

He looked at me.

"Thanks Den, great!"

The bottle glugged as he poured me a glass. He filled everyone else's, then left again and this time returned with two steaming pans, one full to the brim with the glistening freshly cooked pasta, and the other containing a still bubbling sauce made with tomatoes, peppers and herbs. After serving them up he passed round a bowl of grated cheese, then lifted his glass and flashed his eyes at us, laughing.

"Cheers!"

"Cheers!" we returned, and began to eat.

The food was rich and tasty, and to me, extraordinary. I ate and drank with relish. But then – I don't know why it happened as it did – my world became suffused with the utmost horror as I sensed that the spaghetti was of one substance with myself, and alive just as I was. As I bit down on it to chew it, I felt I was chewing living flesh, and that the flesh was squirming and recoiling in pain and fear. A feeling of revulsion instantly came over me, then denial as I tried to shrug it off and hide my shock from my friends. I took a sip of wine, hoping it might relax me and take the edge off the feeling, but now the first shock was followed by another as the wine took on the semblance of warm blood, making me shudder. I put down my glass and tried to compose myself.

"Must use the loo," I muttered, putting my bowl down next to the glass.

"You OK, Ced?" asked Den.

"Fine," I lied. "Caught short."

Get a grip Ced, get a grip. It's just overload. My thoughts were racing. I went up and had a pee, then went to my bedroom and put my face into the pillow and yelled at the top of my voice.

"I'm me! I'm me! I'm me!"

I rolled over on the bed and looked up at the contours of the ceiling mouldings, feeling dazed. I feel picked on, I thought. I feel picked on and reticent, inside out, back to front! I don't stand my ground. I'm on the fucking run! I put my face back into the pillow again.

"I – am – me!" I yelled, my body racked by a furious intent. Then I rolled onto my back again, feeling I'd done something I needed to. I'd said what I'd wanted to say, and had asserted my existence before God and the universe, and felt a determination, felt I had no other choice in fact, than to occupy my place among things and take up my birthright. The sensation that the spaghetti and the wine and my own being, were one substance sharing the same reality, stayed with me, but the sense of horror and what I can only describe as a feeling of cannibalistic transgression, left me. I had a right to be somebody – somebody different – and to eat and drink my fill. The world was mine and I belonged to it. But I was not identical to it. I was different. I was me. I knew it, and I was ready to fight to be me in whatever way I could. I breathed a sigh of relieved satisfaction, then went back downstairs and finished my meal and my glass of wine, still wide-eyed with wonder but at ease with myself and confident that I'd begun to understand the source of the chronic anxiety and panic that had afflicted me over the years, and exhilarated by the knowledge that I had found a way to deal with it.

That evening, Den went with Wendy and a college friend to meet a tutor, and so I gathered up my somewhat sprawling self to go out on my own. There was an event of some kind at a teacher-training college in Heavitree, which might be interesting. So I went. It was the first time since I'd left home that I'd gone out to socialise without having a friend with me or having arranged to meet one. And it felt good – like a treat I'd allowed myself for no other motive than self-love. The place felt exciting and full of promise as I wandered around listening to the din, and looking at all the people under the coloured spotlights with their different clothes and antics, and the film montage projected high up on one of the college walls above the writhing bodies jumping and weaving to the rhythms of the music. I didn't meet anyone that night but was happy just to be there, like someone scuba-diving for the first time and being enthralled by all the exotic colourful life-forms living out their lives in a new and unfamiliar world.

The walk home from Heavitree, though not exhausting, left me feeling relaxed enough to sleep, despite my inner illumination with seemingly perpetual light.
'Perpetual light' – it sounds such a self-evidently good thing when Catholics speak of it in prayer.

"Let your perpetual light shine upon them," they say, their hearts filled with hope for liberation from the darkness of sin.

But the light that I had encountered had been shocking beyond belief. If this had been the face of God, then God was as hellish as he was heavenly. Perpetual light! – no shadows, no privacy, no nooks and crannies to shelter in, no cosy home of one's own. Just the endless brilliance of a consciousness that knows everything – without exception – and in knowing it, possesses it more intimately than one possesses oneself. How can we know it without our own knowledge becoming too great to be contained by our mortal body? The moment I'd first recognised it, I'd known that my mind had been changed forever – that my brain couldn't process it and take hold of it in the usual way – which alas had not stopped me from trying. I'd found, to my horror, that this was not the normal kind of knowledge that one could use to consolidate one's adaptation to the world and incorporate into one's personal bag of manipulative psychological tricks. One could not abuse this conscious presence without knowingly abusing oneself. To know that wherever I turned, this same implacable gaze would be present to my own awareness, was astonishing, marvellous, beautiful, awesome, hideous, devouring, dreadful, absolute, utterly factual, undeniable. Only self-negation and a forgetful diminution of my own knowledge could pretend a denial of sorts, and a superficial respite from the insistent demand that that mere awareness of it now placed upon every scintilla of what I took to be myself:

"Know this – that you, your world, everything that you are, everything that you know and love, even your

knowing itself – you know only because I know you. All that you are is me knowing you knowing yourself."

There were no actual words, but the meaning was crystal clear and overwhelming. Every moment had become decisive – surrender to the simplicity and profundity of this deeply personal revelation of reality, or struggle to ignore it and resurrect that deluded domain in which I felt myself to be king, the apparent sovereign of my own self.

"Christ almighty, Den. I'm cracking up!"
We were sitting in his bedroom in the early afternoon having smoked a couple of joints.
"What's up, man!" he asked.
"Tibetan Book of the Dead – Lord of all Terrors – it's real, Den! I can't do it. I can't do it! I'm fucking cracking up! It's worse than crazy. Crazy would be good! It's nothing compared to this."
"Come on, man. Stop thinking about that stuff. Don't let it get to you. You'll be alright. You've had too much to smoke. Come on, man. Let's go for a walk. We've both had too much."
"Nah, you go Den. I can't. I need to be with this. There isn't any other way for me."
"You sure?" he asked.
"Sure, Den. Don't worry. You're right. I'll be OK."
Whether it was true or not, I knew I'd be better on my own.
Den picked himself up and staggered out of the room.
"OK, I'll see you later," he said.
"Yeah, see you later Den. You take care."

Den wandered down to the river in a daze, barely cognisant of who he was or where he was going, while I just lay there, my head in the pillow, desperately hanging onto my sanity, like someone with no experience of climbing and afraid of heights, poised on the thinnest of toe-holds high up on a cliff face.

10

The weeks which followed the upheaval in my psyche kept alternating between the sublimely beautiful and the ridiculously, ruinously chaotic. And although it was my reading of Janov's book that had originally triggered the episode, I'm quite sure that the constant dope smoking injected an element into it that had nothing to do with childhood primal pain. The psychic overload that cannabis, and before it LSD, had caused, was something new compounded on top of the old. So it wasn't just a case of digging down into the past, bringing it to the surface, feeling it – both sensually and emotionally – and then – hey presto! – the present would take care of itself. No, it was necessary to recognise that the lifestyle I was pursuing was destructive in and of itself, which actually was easier to accomplish when the older stuff was felt and one began to want to care more diligently for oneself again.

To make matters more confusing, it was not just the cannabis consumption that was bringing disorder into my life, but my relationship with Gwen too – which was no more than a concrete consequence of the revolutionary outlook that I had adopted as I entered into adulthood. If Denny had not really grasped the momentous nature of the personal crisis that I'd been going through, how much less did Gwen, who hadn't even been there when it had first erupted? When she returned from her visit to see friends, cultivating further the lifestyle which I was becoming jaded and disillusioned with, I felt impatience and a certain contempt for her. I wanted us to move on. But in those first weeks of what felt like the outcome of something akin in myself to a factory reset, I felt I had been transported to such an altered state of function that I now felt quite alone with little immediate sense of progressing anywhere. I set out on each day with the sense of its being a new adventure, pregnant with every kind of possibility, and by nature uncertain, precarious, daunting, thrilling.

At that time we moved to a bigger house in a rather scruffy Georgian terrace at the entrance to a park in the eastern part of the city. An old friend of Gwen's – Maxim – came one day and never left. He slept on the sofa in the first floor living room. He was short but with broadish shoulders, and had mid-length almond-coloured hair, a full beard, and a ruddy face. He had the wounded awkward manner of someone acutely self-conscious and lacking in self-confidence, and in whose hands things tended almost magically to fall to pieces. Gwen had a soft spot for him and treated him like a pet young brother who needed help tying his shoe laces. She made allowances for the lack of competence which resulted from his lack of confidence. When he amused her with his clumsy ineptness, she didn't judge him, but just laughed affectionately. I regarded him more as just a sometimes amusing, sometimes irritating pet.

His clumsiness extended beyond his body to his intellect, which never seemed to complete a train of thought, making conversation with him an exasperating experience, and true companionship almost unimaginable. And yet he was soft-hearted and sensitive, which made it hard not to like him. And he had a will to live. He got a dog – a lively mongrel, not much older than a pup – which seemed the perfect companion for him. The dog didn't mind at all when he spilt his gravy off his plate, or dropped bits of chicken from his sandwich. It just followed him around, licking the carpet or the linoleum clean after him. They became inseparable until one day a terrible crash and a haunting howl came from the back of the house and I rushed through to find the dog sat upright against a wall of the extension, with a plaintive look on its face and a quiet demeanour. Its hind legs were spread forwards from under it, unnaturally straight and motionless amid a moraine of broken glass that lay beneath an empty frame whose edging of irregular jagged shards were all that was left of the shattered pane that had previously been there. Max had been up at the top of the house playing with the dog. A window had been open, and in a moment of innocent exuberance the dog had leapt through it and fallen three floors down to the ground through the extension roof. Max had rushed down and now came up behind me.

"Oh," he moaned, his voice distraught yet strangely resigned to the calamity. Tears wetted his cheeks and rolled down into his beard. His eyes brimmed and he didn't know what to do with himself, but just kept shifting his slight weight from foot to foot and spreading out his hands, then gripping his head, then his thighs. He bent over the dog and held it like a broken toy that he wanted to put back together again. Wendy came, and then Denny, and we all wanted to comfort Max, who didn't sob because he knew he was clumsy and inept and felt it was surely his fault as it had been so many times before. We all knew that there was really nothing we could do for him. No matter what we said it wouldn't change him. We called a vet, and the vet confirmed that the dog's back was broken and that there was nothing he could do either except put it down. Max knew it had to be done and kneeled down to stroke the dog while the vet injected it and it quietly closed its eyes and slipped away. Max picked up its limp young body and carried it to the vet's car, and could only stand there watching as the car drove off, while Wendy swept up the broken glass, and Denny stuck some bin liners across the hole in the extension roof. I sat on the stairs and cried like a kid while Joni Mitchell's voice singing "My Old Man" drifted down the stairwell from Wendy's room.

It was near the end of the first month in our new house, and we'd been out drinking and playing darts, as we so often did – all of us – Wendy, Phillip, Susie, Den, Gwen and me – Maxim hadn't come yet, and Margot hadn't moved in with us – and the strain of my flagging relationship with Gwen was showing. It wasn't that we became especially angry with each other, or had frequent pyrotechnical spats. Nor did it take the form of a mutual lukewarmness coming over us and dampening our affections for each other. It was more that those affections became increasingly prone to frustration and disappointment, so that we would find ourselves complaining to each other more and more, and arguing over things. The genuineness of our affections made us persist in trying to complete the circle, but no sooner was one gap closed than another opened up.

It didn't come to a tidy end. Rather, one day – this particular day – Gwen's affections for Denny offered a more gratifying prospect than her affections for me. If she'd been hiding her feelings for him from me, she stopped doing so on this day. We'd gone home from the pub and smoked a couple of joints. Phillip and Susie went to bed, then Wendy. But when I wanted to go, Gwen stayed behind in the room with Den. I knew right then that that constant nagging feeling that our previous closeness had essentially been circumstantial, and on her part indulgent in a kind-hearted concessionary kind of way, had been on the mark. I got into bed and waited, and waited. A half hour passed and I began to remember how I'd suffered on account of Nicky's lingering presence. I tried to be patient and strong, but then my strength turned into anger, exasperation and finally a resignation to the fact that I was feeling what, if our relationship had been a truly straight and normal one, would have been a betrayal. I felt I'd had enough and couldn't take any more of it. I jumped out of bed, climbed the stairs heavily, then burst into the living room to find them in each other's arms on the sofa.
"Fuck it!" I shouted. "Fuck it!"
I lashed out with my foot against a holdall on the floor, and kicked it with all my might against one of the walls.
"Oh man," Denny pleaded apologetically.
"Fuck it!" I spat again, then left the room and went back downstairs.

It was quiet for a while as I lay there looking at the sliver of streetlight between the curtains, and the wedge-shaped beam projecting from it that lit up a broad strip running down the wall and across the bed. Then footsteps approached the door, and Gwen and Denny walked in and sat on the floor against the wall.

"I'm sorry, man," Den began.

Gwen stayed silent.

"What shall we do?" he asked.

"Don't know," I replied.

There was a long silence, then I asked, "You want to get in?"

"Is that what you want?" Gwen returned.

"I don' know," I answered – all I knew was that I didn't want to end things with her, and I didn't want to lose my friend either.

They undressed and got into the bed, Gwen lying between us. We lay there unmoving for a while, unsure what to do next, until eventually the absurdity of it got the better of us and Gwen began to laugh, then Den, both of them shaking their heads at the preposterousness of the anti-climax that our actions had led to. I rolled over feeling humiliated and ridiculous, then got up and left to make my bed on the living room floor. The brilliance in my mind was more brilliant than ever. I didn't sob. I didn't weep. I didn't lament as might be expected of a lover who'd lost his sweetheart. Rather, I continued my metamorphosis into a new version of me, the force responsible for it more at the forefront of my mind than my mixed feelings for Gwen. It wasn't that I suddenly stopped wanting her, just that my wanting was not unconditional, and seemed to fuel something much more powerful and profound.

Wendy had heard something of what was going on, and understood enough of it to have more than an inkling of the distress that I must be in. She tapped at the door and pushed it open a little, pushing her head through to peer inside.

"Are you alright, Ced?"

Her concern was genuine.

"Just about," I replied, realising that she'd been listening and already knew that I wasn't really 'alright'.

"D'you want to come to my room?" she asked. "We can talk."

"OK," I answered, grateful for the distraction.

I followed her up the stairs. Her room was lit by a bedside lamp, and there was an opened bottle of red wine on a little table at the foot of the bed.

"What's happening," she inquired, adding hastily, "You don't have to talk about it if you don't want to."

"Nah, it's alright Wendy," I reassured her. "Gwen's with Denny now."

A pained expression took hold of her face.

"Oh, I'm so sorry," she commiserated. "How did that happen?"

"Just did," I explained.

My answer was true, but it hid the history and dynamic of the life we'd been trying to live, and my growing disaffection with it.

She filled my glass, and then her own. She'd already had a few, and her tipsiness made her manner more lugubrious than usual. She was a well-groomed young woman – cultivated – from a loving middle-class home, her face round, kind, generous, gentle, but inclined to blush when she felt put on the spot.

"I need to get away," I said to her. "Go live on my own somewhere."

"But you're so sociable, Ced," she protested. "You mustn't!"
"Yeah, I think I need to, Wendy. I need to get myself together. I can't do this anymore. I've changed. If you could see what was going on in my mind, you wouldn't believe it."
"What do you mean Ced?"
"I mean, if you could see it you'd think I was crazy! It's unbelievable! It's not just to do with Gwen. I'm not the way I was. She doesn't know who I am now."
"But we all change, don't we Ced?"
"Well, yeah. But not like this! This is different altogether!"
"Can I help?" she asked, leaning towards me.
The way she looked at me, I realised that in the nicest of ways she was offering herself to me, body as well as mind. At any other time I think flattery would have got the better of me, but in these few moments, after at first feeling a certain obligation to return her kindness, I realised I felt no sexual desire for her and didn't have the heart to fake it. I reached over to touch her hand, but she understood immediately that it was a rejection, and then flushed with awkward embarrassment and ashamed annoyance at having dared to expose her heart in so defenceless a way.
"I'm sorry," she said, drawing her hand away. "It was silly of me."
"No Wendy, don't. It's not you. It's me. I'm in a state! I'm no good to anybody at the moment."
I wanted to take her self-reproach away from her, and took responsibility for her failed effort upon myself. Then I caressed her as she lay back upon the bed, sliding through my arms until my head rested on her tummy. I think she'd long wanted Den and was disappointed too by this turn of events. I think she'd wanted *him* to want her body and now

just wanted *someone* to want it. It had been a fair bid, even though she'd probably known in her heart that it would be a futile one. And so she lay there, her sadness subdued as she sank into sleep with her hand on my crown and my arm wrapped around her hip. The alcohol soothed both of our nerves, enough to rest mine briefly in the solar flood that was deluging my inner vision. Outside I heard thunder rumbling in the distance again, as it had when I'd last endured a calamitous change in my personal stasis, and began to wonder if it was just coincidence or something deeper.

We carry on, don't we? As long as there's a drop or a flicker of life left in us, no matter how dissembled the wreckage of our lives may have become, that drop or flicker wants more life. For it, suicide is never an option. Only our egos commit our bodies to suicide. Bodies themselves never do. No matter how wounded or tortured by circumstances they are, they always remain faithful to the value of life. That's why our egos can be tortured – the true self is unconditionally committed to life for as long as it remains alive – something that is a scandal and a bane to the ego, which always, it seems, feels life is only worth living if it is destined for pleasure and happiness. The true self doesn't live like that. It just strives to live, no matter what. Only death itself brings the self's commitment to an end, never just the perhaps comforting *thought* of death, unless the ego rebels against the self and takes the easy way out.

Around that time we'd been listening to Pink Floyd's 'Dark Side of the Moon' a lot, and its focus on sanity and madness had felt particularly poignant for me, making listening to it a strange blend of ecstatic pleasure and anguish. My own sanity felt so intense that I could hardly bear it and wondered if it was real or not. It seemed hardly possible that ordinary life could be experienced like this. After what happened with Gwen, I spent days wandering on my own around the city's parks and streets, just marvelling at the sheer beauty and the immediate satisfaction of my simple perceptions of things, and all the while, between the spells of sunshine, my experience seemed to be accompanied by dramatic displays of thunder and lightning, which began to feel uncanny and mysterious, even as I questioned my imaginings as products of my own fanciful musing. I found solace in one of the trees in the park next to the terrace, and often went out when the evenings began to feel too long, to seek courage and support in the firm press of my body against its irregular corrugated bark. I would stretch my arms around its girth that I might be as close as I possibly could to its stoutness and dependability, seeking the safety of its fraternal shelter, and willing that its strength might enter into me.

Back at the house some weeks later, we had a guest came to stay – a friend of Gwen's who came from Folkestone. From the moment I first met him, I felt repelled by him. I couldn't explain it to myself to begin with, and I did my best to be polite and pleasant towards him, but it was a visceral feeling of intense revulsion at something about him that flatly contradicted my deepest sense of life's meaning. He was tall, slim, had fairish hair, and wore glasses. When I think of Wendy and her tendency to blush, which evoked a sense of childish transparency and the nervous palpability of life animating the flesh right through to the body's surface, then I begin to get a sense of what so recoiled me about Matthew: in him, while there was intellect and wit, and deep movement of the body, at the surface there was nothing. His skin seemed ashen, and the drab clothes and the brown beret that he wore, seemed to perfectly complete the picture of someone in whom life had taken a leave of absence. In him it was as if a spirit were labouring to animate a corpse rather than incarnating itself in a body of its own. He appeared as borrowed flesh to me, and I truly wished that he would leave. It seemed unkind to feel that way, however, and so I forced myself to accommodate him for the few days that he stayed. And I was grateful to him at least for putting my own trials into perspective. Eventually, after a daily succession of heroic but doomed attempts at light-hearted entertainment, he went back to what I insincerely imagined must be a box of earth in the crypt of a derelict abbey in Folkestone, and breathed a sigh of relief as the atmosphere perceptibly lightened, and Den and I exchanged knowing looks behind Gwen's back whenever his name was mentioned.

Despite the turnaround in our respective fortunes regarding Gwen, my bond of friendship with Den remained firm and warm, and I was still the bookish, idealistic high-flyer who Gwen turned to for intellectual stimulation and occasional sex, while he stayed solid, masculine and workmanlike in his pursuit of sculptural beauty. Max, who was living with us by now, remained reliably inept and unreliable in his inimical amiable way, and Susie continued loyally to be Phillip's pillar of companionable support in his reverse through life one sober step forward and two drunken ones back. Wendy brought her wholesome humanity to every occasion, while we all struck out on the paths which, without quite realising it in those days of chance discovery and glorious unpredictability, would already set us on the courses that would define us as the more or less mature people that we would eventually become.

As the days began to bring signs of the coming autumn, our lease on the place, along with the summer, approached its end. In due course Den, Gwen, Phillip and Susie moved back to Western Road, while Wendy moved in with some new college friends. And in an unlikely pairing, Max and I moved out to a shack on Haldon Hill five miles outside the city. The hill with its three-cornered tower, and the scrubby, lightly forested ridge leading to it, overlooked Exeter from the west, the magnificent vista stretching down across the luxuriant farm land of the Exe vale, all the way to the estuary at Exmouth. Some months later we learned that Matthew had thrown himself under a commuter train speeding towards London. He'd been decapitated

www.ingramcontent.com/pod-product-compliance
Lightning Source LLC
Chambersburg PA
CBHW031444040426
42444CB00007B/968